W9-BUV-039

"For the last twenty years, Martha Alderson has created invaluable, popular tools to help writers understand the essential components of plot development and storytelling. Now, in *Boundless Creativity*, she brilliantly applies the principles illuminated in her breakthrough book, *The Plot Whisperer*, to the creative process. In this clear, inspiring workbook, Alderson lays out the spiritual voyage to higher creativity—illuminating a clear path to inspire and guide anyone with even the hint of a creative dream. If you want to successfully navigate the highs and lows of living a creative life, you'll want this book as an essential companion."

—**Laura Davis**, coauthor of *The Courage to Heal*, author of *I Thought We'd Never Speak Again* and *Wholehearted*, and founder of The Writer's Journey workshops

"Martha Alderson's new book is an indispensable creative coach whispering, 'Keep going,' on every page."

—**Holly Lynn Payne**, novelist, screenwriter, and founder of Booxby

"Open-minded individuals looking for a road map to realize their creative potential will find this and more within the pages of *Boundless Creativity*. Prepare for a deep dive within to answer questions about personal fears, misbeliefs, and the origins of self-doubt that may be holding you back, and then learn how to let go of it to live your best creative life."

—**Angela Ackerman**, coauthor of *The Emotion Thesaurus*

"A brilliant, thought-provoking resource that serves not only as an inspiration for creative projects, but also as a meditation for writers, filmmakers, and artists ready to dive deep, overcome challenges, and produce their best work. The Plot Whisperer has done it again!"

—**Hallee Adelman, PhD**, author of *Way Past Mad*, and producer/director of *Our American Family*

"In *Boundless Creativity*, Martha Alderson offers an inspiring, much-needed pattern for realizing our creative goals. By aligning our planning with the steps of the Universal Story, she guides us through the pitfalls and triumphs we artists experience as we travel down to the dark caverns and up to the light pinnacles of our creative dreams. Not only does the author share her own revelations, she coaches us through the fears and triumphs we all face while planning and executing a work of art. A workbook to prize, useful for creatives and workshop leaders, as we aim toward personal and professional fulfillment."

—**Gini Grossenbacher, MEd**, award-winning author of *Madam of My Heart* and *Madam in Silk*; editor; speaker; JGKS Press publisher; and director of Elk Grove Writers and Artists, an AWA affiliate

"*Boundless Creativity* demystifies and normalizes the highs and lows of the creative lifecycle. Through a transformational program that Alderson compares to alchemy—'A ritual of subjecting base metals (the imperfect individual) to scorching fire (challenges and change), burning off the dross (burdens and flaws) and transforming into gold (the fully realized individual)'—she guides us to identify and defang the demons that suck us into that familiar tar pit of self-doubt and creative paralysis. No matter your medium—driftwood, paints, musical notes, flour/flowers, words—*Boundless Creativity* will lead you back to your belief in the miraculous. Back to your belief in yourself."

—**Elaine Taylor**, founder of the nonprofit, The Grief Relief Project, for people poleaxed by loss; and author of *Karma Deception and a Pair of Red Ferraris*

Boundless Creativity

A SPIRITUAL WORKBOOK for OVERCOMING SELF-DOUBT, EMOTIONAL TRAPS, and OTHER CREATIVE BLOCKS

MARTHA ALDERSON, MA

REVEAL PRESS

AN IMPRINT OF NEW HARBINGER PUBLICATIONS

Publisher's Note

This publication is designed to provide accurate and authoritative information in regard to the subject matter covered. It is sold with the understanding that the publisher is not engaged in rendering psychological, financial, legal, or other professional services. If expert assistance or counseling is needed, the services of a competent professional should be sought.

Distributed in Canada by Raincoast Books

Copyright © 2020 by Martha Alderson
           Reveal Press
           An imprint of New Harbinger Publications, Inc.
           5674 Shattuck Avenue
           Oakland, CA 94609
           www.newharbinger.com

Cover design by Amy Daniel

Acquired by Elizabeth Hollis Hansen

Edited by Jennifer Eastman

All Rights Reserved

Library of Congress Cataloging-in-Publication Data on file

Printed in the United States of America

22   21   20

10   9   8   7   6   5   4   3   2   1   First Printing

To Luisa

Contents

Phase 4: The Prize

Welcome to Your Best Creative Life
Through the Universal Story

Are you intrigued by the idea of living a spiritually and emotionally satisfying creative life? Perhaps your imagination vibrates with excitement, but you don't know where to begin. You're bored and ready—even desperate—to enliven your life. Maybe you're a writer who shows up to write every day but often feels blocked. Or you're a painter whose trek of living up to everyone else's expectations leaves you yearning for your true purpose. Depressed in the mire of routine, you don't believe you're imaginative and brave enough to live an artful and joyful life. Or you're content with your life...*thank you very much*. Dive a bit deeper. I bet that while your mind and habits fight to remain the same, your heart and vision root for change.

Boundless Creativity seeks to change your perception of life from a place of self-doubt and stuck patterns into a series of creative breakthroughs. Our spiritual nature is to embrace creativity, just as all of life is made up of creative energy. Throughout this workbook, you're invited to cross over from passive reader to active creative or maker by answering questions, performing exercises, and completing a creative project. For example, before we go any further, you have a decision to make.

Are you willing to risk changing in meaningful ways to live your best creative life? Circle your answer.

Yes   *No*

By personally interacting with the material in this way, you pull ideas and beliefs from your mind into your body as you take action, circling and writing and creating something new.

When asked if they were currently living their best life, a group of creatives I surveyed responded no far more than yes. Those who answered no expressed a variety of missing factors. Confidence, self-worth, and time topped the list. One creative cited a need for outside help.

"A housekeeper and cook, a nest egg, and dogs and kids who leave me alone. I'm serious!"

How about you? Are you living your best creative life now?

Yes   *No*

Take a moment to draw or write what living your best creative life looks like, even if only in your imagination.

A MYSTICAL BOND

Creativity connects us to our spirit. You're writing a difficult scene and suddenly the exact right word pops in your mind. An unexpected refund check arrives in the mail with enough money to pay for that new easel you were convinced you couldn't afford. You need help with a project, the phone rings, and the person you want is on the other end. Are these simply remarkable coincidences, or is something else involved?

When the lines of communication with our spirit are open and free flowing, we have access to an endless supply of energy and support. Yet if we haven't already completely forgotten about our wonder, all too often, the static weight of our emotional history causes us to struggle to realize our artistic ambitions and live our best creative life.

I don't think there's ever been a time when I haven't felt part of a spiritual bond that has nothing to do with the intellect or the rational and everything to do with intuition, imagination, creativity, and trust, but my relationship to the mystery was much clearer and more absorbing when I was child. Then, I didn't question the awareness; I simply believed. Doubts crept in as I attended school, suffered pain and betrayal, and matured.

> *"If it can't be perceived by the traditionally recognized five senses of taste, smell, touch, hearing, and sight, it's simply a hunch and not real."*

> *"If you can't prove your intuitive awareness scientifically, then it's nothing more than magical thinking."*

But despite these doubts, the truth is that the knowing never left me.

What inner truth or knowing about yourself and how you view life has never left you?

_____

_____

_____

These days, I'm known as the Plot Whisperer for my work supporting writers and artists and extraordinary people from five years old to 102. I started out whispering plot support to writers and quickly found that the universal story at the core of every great book reaches beyond characters and writing into the very lives of the writers imagining the fictional tales. Now I help creatives of every ilk plot their own artful trajectory to creative success. My whispering as much benefits the artist as the art they produce.

My intention in writing _Boundless Creativity_ is to share secrets I've gleaned from thirty years of studying stories and exploring creatives' relationships with their art through interviews, consultations, surveys, and field notes. I want to give you the means to turn what's right in front of you upside down. Cultivate emotions that thrust you forward and weed out those that block your light. Translate what your spirit and creativity are trying to teach you about your life.

Do you currently consider yourself a creative person?   _Yes_   _No_

If yes, what is (or are) your preferred medium (media) of expression?

_____

_____

_____

INNER AND OUTER DISCOVERY

If you're like me, when you read an inspirational book, you write down quotes, highlight sections, and stick reminders everywhere. Then, over time, your enthusiasm fades into everyday living. Before long, you fail to remember the help. This is common, because true and lasting growth demands action.

In this workbook, you're asked to create something of your choosing while simultaneously tracking your inner life, your energy, emotions, beliefs, habits, and traits. Traveling through each of four phases and twenty steps won't land you in the middle of your best creative life all at once, suddenly rid of your doubts and negative emotions. You will, however, be changed in ways you never imagined.

Boundless Creativity travels along two tiers to connect you to your spirit and fire your enthusiasm for creativity. The creative layer involves plotting and enacting steps to achieve your outer creative goals. Action moves esoteric concepts into your muscle memory and allows transformation to begin. In the process, you unearth your spirit. Your outer creativity path is intrinsically linked to your inner spiritual purpose and potential.

You give yourself a goal and immediately confront yourself—your abilities, strengths, weaknesses, resistance, and struggle. You come face-to-face with your dreams and fears, your patterns and flaws, your supporters and foes. The spiritual layer of the program curls around your thoughts and beliefs, intuition and imagination to reawaken your earliest wisdom and belief that anything is possible. It breathes new life in to your actions and reawakens childlike wonder and inner peace.

When was the last time you felt childlike wonder?

_____

_____

What elicited the wonder?

_____

_____

When did you last feel inner peace?

_____

_____

What elicits peace within you?

_____

_____

Together, outer success and inner joy add up to a transcendent life.

RESTORE COMMUNICATION

Each chapter in *Boundless Creativity* represents a step in our program. Throughout the steps, you're offered prompts, in the form of questions, to reflect on the page and reintroduce you to the language of your spirit. At the end of each step, a section called "Take Action" spurs your pursuit of an external creativity goal. Each step builds on the previous one.

Think of this workbook as a journal-guide in which you uncover and explore thoughts and feelings surrounding your pursuit of creativity. A mindful practice of untangling your beliefs invites you to explore memories long buried, truths you didn't know you held, and emotions that control you. Connecting to yourself more deeply through self-reflection often reveals surprising results.

Inner strength and belief lead you to achieve your external creativity goal and, at the same time, open access to even more creativity and vitality in your life. They help you discover your own personal spiritual trip as it aligns with your outer path to creativity, celebrate the natural rhythm of your everyday life, and adjust what isn't working. The deeper you travel into the mystery, the more you appreciate your growing and changing. In the end, you know yourself, and those around you, better. You heal and forgive, grow and transform, gain courage and acceptance, and enjoy every day more creatively.

"I show up for regular exercise. I show up to feed my body. And I show up to feed my creativity.
It's a bit like combing my hair and brushing my teeth, I feel off if I'm not doing it regularly."

Transformation happens in the doing, by actively shedding the old and seeking change. Yet, all too often, the fantastical ideas we dream up fade over time due to a lack of will, a lack of attention, or a lack of belief. One artist I worked with started our first session by describing her latest project. Only minutes into her explanation, she laughed nervously and berated her ideas as being too "out there" and too "crazy." She began with such promise, but suddenly lost her confidence and the meaning in her vision. To be successful in creating something out of nothing and manifest her concept of the unseen world, she had work to do. We all do.

Without thinking, describe the internal work you may need to do to bring what's in your imagination out into the world.

THE BENEFITS OF LIVING A CREATIVE LIFE

Each of us has a creative purpose to honor and fulfill. Don't turn away because you think your dream is impossible. The odyssey itself is the treasure.

Creativity invites you every day and in every moment to see the world anew. Time expands in unexplainable ways. Little parts inexplicably click into place as your life begins to shape itself around your dreams. You surprise yourself by intuitively looking up just as an eagle glides across the sky or a humpback whale breaches in the bay, and once again, you're inspired to create.

Write down your earliest and fondest memory that involves creating, making, constructing, inventing, or designing something new.

_____

_____

_____

_____

_____

When we're young, as if by an invisible umbilical cord, we're connected to the great beyond. As we grow up, it's easy to become so caught up in fear or in trying to keep up that we disconnect from our lifeline to the miraculous and miss the wildness, the joy, and the freedom in every breath.

You find yourself saying, *I've always wanted…* Fill in the blank.

_____

_____

_____

Boundless Creativity moves you from where you are currently to where you want to be and to who you wish to become.

UNIVERSAL STORY ESSENTIALS

Living your best creative life takes you on a spiritual quest that is often deep and profound. The map to reclaiming a sense of possibilities in the miraculous is the Universal Story—an energetic pathway that runs throughout our lives and all of nature with the promise of transformation. I've written books about the Universal Story as it applies to writing and characters. But as I worked on these books, I began to realize that the pattern running through stories pours throughout all life. Your spirit is your life force tucked in the heartbeat of the Universal Story.

Boundless Creativity taps into the Universal Story to better direct the flow of your life and connect you to your creative promise. Awareness of the Universal Story will expand your everyday life. Be forewarned! It can also drastically change the person you are now as you step into who you came here to be.

What habits and beliefs and skills of yours fit the image you have of living your best creative life?

_____

_____

_____

_____

_____

ORIGINS OF THE UNIVERSAL STORY

I came to writing late. Nonverbal and dyslexic as a child, I hid in my imagination. Daydreaming and reading stories all day long and deep into the night is quite different from writing them down. First, I became a speech pathologist and learning specialist, and opened a speech, language, and learning disability clinic for children. When I was nearly forty, I sold my practice and started writing fiction. Plot—a critical element in all great stories—challenged me. After analyzing countless prize-winning and classic stories, I grasped the concept. Writer friends started asking me to teach them what I was learning.

With my special education background, I created visual templates to show plot. I learn best through a multisensory approach of seeing, hearing, and manipulating new material. I believe we all unravel and integrate esoteric concepts more easily that way.

One of the templates I created was an attempt to make visible the energetic structure of stories, which I call the Plot Planner. A story's energy isn't flat. The line reflects how the momentum rises and where the energy is likely to fall and then rush to a conclusion.

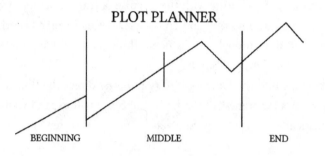

I divided the line into four equal parts to honor how the heart of every story entails twice the effort as beginnings and endings do. In every Plot Planner I created for the stories I analyzed, wrote, and was consulted about, the Universal Story stared back at me—a universal heartbeat with no beginning and no end.

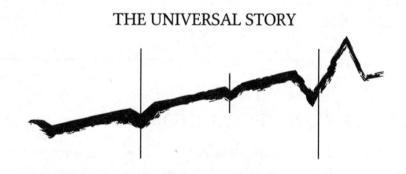

Don't be fooled into believing that because the visual representation of the energy of the Universal Story looks simple it doesn't exist. Simplicity is one of those paradoxes in life; what appears grand and important is an illusion, and that which is small and seemingly insignificant is everything.

Fascination with Energy

I've had a lifelong desire to understand two things: energy and emotions. What causes our personal energy to soar, and why does it plummet? Who has suffered, and what choices do they make as a result? What draws people to venture beyond the safety of how things have always been done? Why do some dreams die while others come true with little effort?

I was repeatedly molested as a young girl. Developmentally delayed, I didn't have the words to speak about what was happening to me. As a result, I spent most of my twenties and thirties as a victim. I blamed and shamed myself unmercifully. Before long, other victims began showing up in my life. Rather than rise up together in strength, we seemed to withdraw into tiny boxes—listless, frightened, and self-destructive.

Desperate to ignite my nerve, I studied the energy systems in our bodies, the healing power of energy work and the energy of the spirit. Determined to move beyond self-imposed limitations, I also earned a degree in psychology in college—and later a master's degree in communication—studying the emotional reactions of people seemingly unencumbered by the pain of the past, people who were creative, energetic, and successful without losing themselves in the process or resorting to bullying and hurting others.

By the time I embraced the Universal Story, I'd worked my way out of the hole I'd been tossed into as a kid. That didn't mean I was no longer attacked by fear or completely rid of my detrimental tendencies, but I'd let in the light.

The Light

The Universal Story's energy spoke to me as what had been blurry began to clear. Awareness of this energetic pattern flung open doors to reveal the meaning of my struggles, beliefs, friends, family, and everything that had been right in front of me all along. The pattern of contraction and flow of the Universal Story, like our heartbeat, has significance within itself and to the whole.

The Universal Story points out the moment you move from talking about what you want in life to going after it. The Universal Story highlights when you persevere even in the face of certain disaster—and prevail. The more you appreciate the basic rhythm of the Universal Story, the closer attention you give to the choices you make, the words you speak, and the schedules you create.

What do you want in life?

_____

_____

_____

_____

_____

Are you currently in active pursuit of that desire?   *Yes*   *No*

Boundless Creativity is out to save high hopes and noble goals that until now have been unrealized and unexpressed. The Universal Story is the X-marks-the-spot treasure map how to get there.

THE FOUR PHASES OF THE UNIVERSAL STORY

Creating something real and tangible from your imagination—a story, a painting, a song, a film, a lovely home, or simply doing something old in a fresh new way—while keeping your spiritual journey front and center introduces obstacles that must be overcome. Many of these setbacks are predetermined and arrive at specific moments in every undertaking to signal

- where you are on your way to success,

- what is likely to derail you, and

- the necessary skills and abilities you need to flourish.

Mastery moves you through the four phases toward that which you most desire.

The Universal Story, the format of this workbook, and every creative endeavor are divided into four major phases—idea, action, adversity, and success—that I translate into "Know Yourself," "Sea of Creativity," "Dive Deep," and "The Prize." Each of these four phases carries its own kind of energy meant to challenge the habits of your mind and your personality.

Choosing to live a creative life entails facing a constant dare: will you play it safe or steadfastly move forward? The Universal Story is littered with markers warning you where to adjust for a new rhythm. It points out resting places to help you stick with it even when you no longer trust your vision, when you've fallen out of love with what you're creating, and when your commitment to continue on—no matter what comes—is rapidly slipping away. Through it all, you radiate joy and grace living a creative life, knowing change is born of challenges.

Energy Markers

Writers show the journey their characters undertake in their stories. But if you think of yourself as the hero of *your* story, it becomes possible to stand back and view your victories and demons as scenes and characters in your own mystical odyssey. Identify life-changing energy markers for a better understanding of how you arrived at where you are and how to better direct your way forward.

First, before you identify the major markers in your life, familiarize yourself with what each phase and marker in the Universal Story represents symbolically. If you're a creative person looking to more fully embrace your creativity, record the times you tried something new. If creativity hasn't played a big part in your life until now, look for energy markers in your overall life experiences.

In each of the four phases, the energy surges to a major energy marker where a decision waits—will you cross the threshold to the next phase or stop where you are?

What Shook Your Spirit?

As you complete the next exercise, look for events that shook your spirit—that radiant part of you. Include setbacks that came out of hardship. We are not changed through our successes. Rather, it is disasters and crisis, adversity and loss, disappointment and hurt that define our potential to transform.

If an art piece was particularly challenging, and you had to stretch and often suffer criticism and rejection, include it. You got married and lived happily ever, don't include it. You got married and found yourself challenged in ways you never imagined, include it. You wrote a short story that won a Pushcart Prize, don't include it. You tried writing a short story, never finished it and still think about it, include it.

The reason your successes don't have a place in the exercises below is because when you're comfortable, you rarely change. Challenges, so-called failures, and mistakes hold secret purposes and carry messages about where you are in the Universal Story. As the veils of protection fall away, your heart begins to express its special and unique qualities and creativity.

READY TO BEGIN?

If you're ready to get started, record today's date.

Today's Date   _____

Four Phases and Four Energy Markers

Following are the four phases of the Universal Story along with their accompanying energy markers.

THE UNIVERSAL STORY

NO TURNING BACK

Know
Yourself

KNOW YOURSELF

Beginnings make up phase 1 of the Universal Story, with the promise of something new. The energy of the beginning builds to the energy marker at the end of the beginning of any endeavor—No Turning Back. This is a moment of breaking away from all that is expected of you and setting out on your own.

Below, list any time you felt pulled, thrown, dragged away from the life you've always known. Mention if you willingly left with gusto or were pushed or squeezed out of what was familiar and into a mystery. Note when you willingly or unwillingly left a place of safety and took an unexpected risk to start a new creativity project. Indicate how your actions worked out.

_____

_____

_____

_____

_____

_____

If you haven't met any challenges or acted on behalf of a creative idea because you've been afraid to rock the boat, you're likely trapped in the beginning of the Universal Story.

THE UNIVERSAL STORY

RECOMMITMENT

Sea of
Creativity

THE SEA OF CREATIVITY

In phase 2 of the Universal Story, the nearer you sail toward your goals and dreams and passions, the more resistance you face. Each time you set out to accomplish something concrete and measurable is like participating in an initiation or a rite of passage. Opposition, both external and internal, appears from every angle. Then, nearly halfway to your goal, your enthusiasm drains. This predictable energy marker—Recommitment—arrives when you suddenly bump into what appears to be an insurmountable problem, become ensnarled in a misunderstanding, are overcome with exhaustion, or confront a foe. The energy around you intensifies.

Below, list the times you were consumed by angst, pursued by demons, embroiled in drama, entangled in setbacks, and felt challenged in life—when every forward action was met with pushback, or when, in the midst of creating something new, you faltered.

Now, the question: did you persevere or retreat?   *Persevere*   *Retreat*

Put a star next to the memories you listed above when you rededicated yourself to your dreams and desires even when faced with stiff opposition. Indicate how your convictions worked out for you.

_____

_____

_____

_____

_____

THE UNIVERSAL STORY

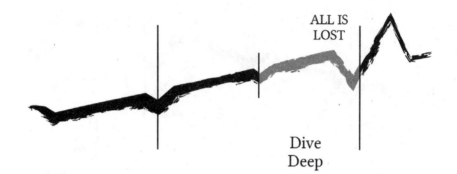

DIVE DEEP

During the third phase of the Universal Story, you're met with a series of obstacles designed to test you and turn your life around. Your emotional maturity is challenged. Outgrown beliefs backfire. Weaknesses are exposed. You're embarrassed, publically humiliated, dishonored. The energy marker in Dive Deep—All Is Lost—is a dark night of the soul, hell on earth, a breakdown and crisis.

All-is-lost is a life-or-death turning point in the Universal Story. This is where you die to all you know and lose all you hold dear. Stripped bare, people in crisis are lost and traumatized with no belief left. Here, where the stakes are at their highest, you can remain reeling for hours or for a lifetime. Or, with the courage and insight found in the Universal Story, risk everything for your dreams and your spirit. If you survive the collision, surprise attack, and heartache, you prove you're worthy of the prize.

Now, examine moments and events that you may otherwise wish to forget. These are times when everything went bleak and black in your life. When have you lost your way, were deceived, broken, and left for dead? What happened next?

_____

_____

_____

_____

_____

THE UNIVERSAL STORY

TRIUMPH

The
Prize

THE PRIZE

The fourth phase of the Universal Story is a time of triumphing over the last giant waves and life-threatening riptides to seize the prize—both external success and spiritual wisdom. After the all-is-lost death in phase 3, you're reborn and see life from an entirely new perspective. Knowledge and insight are gained at the fourth energetic marker—Triumph. Your intuition is awakened. You have greater perception and develop new powers of imagination and creativity. This is a time of achievement, climax, change, and transformation.

What are your greatest successes that came out of great struggle and pain? What happened next?

_____

_____

_____

_____

_____

HOW TO USE THE UNIVERSAL STORY

The Universal Story is your map and itinerary throughout this voyage. Refer to it for a sense of where you're headed with your creativity and where you currently stand in your life. Anticipate what comes next and glean a sense of the energy required of you as you dive deeper and deeper into the very heart of you.

As the energy of the Universal Story intensifies, you're faced with tests that assess your strengths and readiness for success and that show which of your skills and abilities fall short. Trials for spiritual growth wait as long as it takes for you to say yes to change. Track your progress against the Universal Story as you actively pursue your creative goals. Rather than wait for something creative to magically appear, take matters into your own hands.

If you knew you would succeed, what creativity goals would you set for yourself?

_____

_____

_____

_____

_____

_____

_____

_____

To achieve your creativity goals, follow the rhythm of the Universal Story. A view of your entire plan emerges along with a better understanding of the significance of each of its parts. With such an insight, you're able to turn actions with emotionally rich meaning into the driving force behind an exceptional life. The ability to live in the current moment is key to spiritual evolution. So, too, is the ability to stand back and grasp the whole.

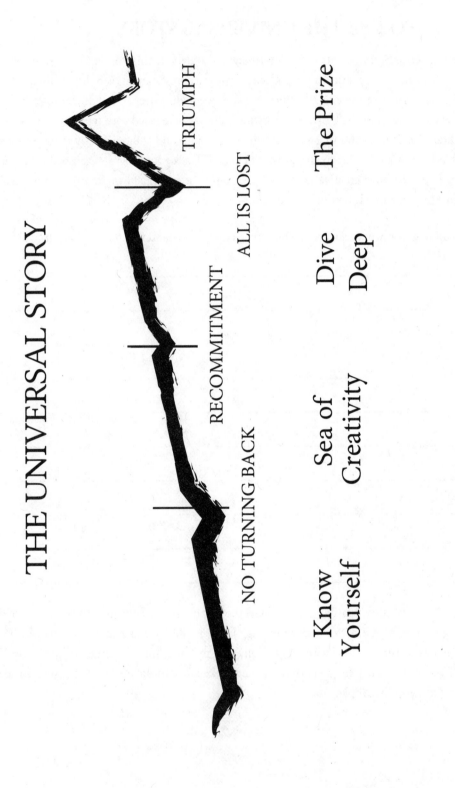

THE UNIVERSAL STORY

TRIUMPH

ALL IS LOST

RECOMMITMENT

NO TURNING BACK

Know
Yourself

Sea of
Creativity

Dive
Deep

The Prize

PHASE 1

Know
Yourself

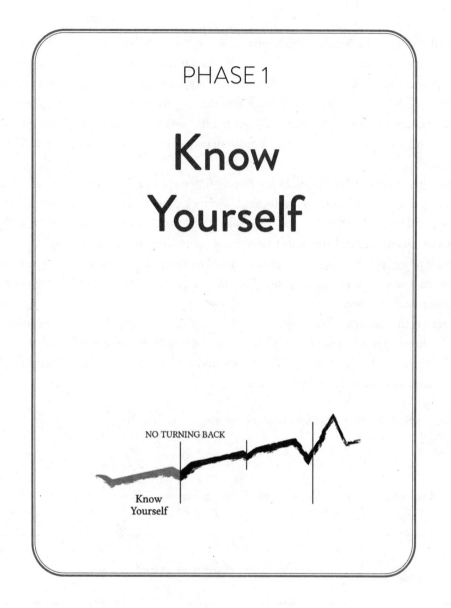

NO TURNING BACK

Know
Yourself

The spiritual voyage to higher creativity starts at Know Yourself. Though fragile, beginnings embody great heart and hope. In this phase, we explore your relationship to creativity as it stands now.

The energy of the Universal Story to self-understanding forms gradually and nonthreateningly as you travel through both inner and outer realities. Zoom through the material or meander; you control the speed for your course of action. One course doesn't fit all. And one course doesn't last a lifetime. You can switch direction anytime you choose, opt for a different path. The only way you can't go is back to the way things were.

We're often a mystery to ourselves. What usually first comes when doing the workbook exercises is your surface truth—what you've been taught, read, and picked up from others, an easy one-off. The more time you schedule for self-reflection and self-exploration, the deeper you dive through illusions and misperceptions, shame and embarrassment to arrive at your own personal truth.

There are no right or wrong answers and emotional reactions to the questions and prompts scattered throughout the four phases of this program. They are simply your answers and emotional reactions to record, witness, and compare.

The truth is that you're always creating and changing and evolving. This program empowers you to intentionally direct your adjustments. Ultimately, your inner spirit comes together with your outer work. Unified, the two paths become an expression of joy and success. Consciously or unconsciously, and in whichever direction, the universal rhythm remains.

Can you see committing to a creativity goal all the way through to the end, no matter what comes?

Yes   *No*

If you circled no, what needs to change so you'll say yes?

STEP 1

Dreams and Desires and the Value of Living a Creative Life

My mother dominated my early life. And creativity dominated her entire life. One of the greatest gifts she gave me was modeling one way to live a creative life. I don't remember a time she wasn't driven to create—paint a portrait to hang at the de Young Art Museum, or a landscape or a still life; cook holiday dinners to be shared at our table with servicemen stationed at a nearby military base; knit matching sweaters for my siblings and me and even my favorite doll; weave lace and wall hangings; form pique assiette mosaics and chess pieces from clay for the church bazaar; paint on silk and on rocks; decorate handmade porcelain tiles; imitate paintings by old masters in needlepoint and textiles. Then, one day when she was ninety-five years old, her hands lay still in her lap. Two days later, she was dead.

The highs of her perceived creative success lit up her face as she read feature articles about herself in local newspapers and accepted commissions for paintings. At those times, she exuded confidence in her creativity. She'd point out shadows created by live oak trees sprawled across straw-colored hills where I saw footprints of passing giants. As a fundraiser for my high school, she organized art shows by Bay Area artists soon to become famous—Diebenkorn, Wonner, and Thiebaud. Sewing classes taught by my mother were traded with cooking classes taught by a Cordon Bleu chef, the mother of my best friend.

My mother was also crushed by perceived failures. Her eyes and lips turned down after hours of coaxing colors to conform to outsiders' input about a painting, now a muddy mess. There were pieces she abandoned because of criticism. Her energy would plummet, and she'd retreat to lie alone in the dark. At those times, the entire house was plunged into uncertainty and silence until one of us—usually me—was pushed into her bedroom, apologized for some undefined slight, and reassured her of our love.

When I started writing fiction, I became determined to create techniques of acceptance to mitigate the lows of living a creative life without dampening the highs. As I integrated more and more creativity into my life, I found myself experiencing the familiar mood swings I'd grown up absorbing from my mother. Rather than succumb to the roller coaster of emotions, I experimented, lived and probed, researched and studied the Universal Story and the process of creativity. This workbook is my love letter to you, showing you how not only to survive the ups and downs of living your best creative life…but also to thrive.

How often did creativity appear in your childhood?

Always   *Often*   *Seldom*   *Never*

Explain your answer.

_____

_____

_____

What creative activities did you enjoy the most?

_____

_____

_____

WHAT IS CREATIVITY?

"Spiritual" relates to the inner you. Your strength and vitality emanate from your spirit. One way to celebrate and nurture your spirit is through creativity. Spirit and creativity intertwine and become one as creativity turns spirit into an artistic work and sensory reality.

Have you experienced moments of awe, when you felt absolutely no struggle, no thought, and you were simply a silent creator letting creativity flow into the physical world?

Yes   *No*

If not, you soon will.

Creativity allows you to experience your spirit through your six senses—sight, smell, touch, hearing, taste, and the extrasensory intuition and perception of knowing without knowing why. You may sense

- the warmth of a stone sculpture,

- the rusty smell of oil paint on canvas,

- the cinnamon taste of an apple cobbler,

- the shifting sound of a foghorn, or

- a sunlit rose promising spring.

What sensual experiences have connected you to your creativity or inspired a yearning to be creative?

_____

_____

_____

_____

Embracing a Life of Creativity

Creativity is an inclination, an impulse, and a tendency. Creative practices like writing and studying the Universal Story offer opportunities to step away from your everyday reality and develop your inner spiritual life. Create something out of nothing but your imagination and gain a new sense of yourself.

Art is a way to communicate. Whatever your creative medium, telling a story or painting a portrait, designing a garden or performing an interpretive dance, you're artfully expressing yourself. What you have to say deserves to be heard. What you create changes the future. Creativity awakens us in the moment and brings value and meaning to every aspect of our lives.

List the benefits you receive or believe you'll receive by fulfilling your creativity goals and living a creative life.

_____

_____

_____

_____

When surveyed, a random sample of creatives list the five top benefits they receive from fulfilling their creativity goals and living a creative life:

- joy
- belief
- peace of mind

- sanity
- self-respect

Reasons to Be Creative

People create for all sorts of reasons—for money, for fame, as a hobby, as a form of activism, as a way of life, and as means of giving in to a vision, a whisper, a line of dialogue, a series of notes, or an imagined world.

List your reasons for wanting to live a creative life.

_____

_____

_____

_____

_____

_____

Whatever your personal reasons are, throughout this workbook, you're asked to create as a way to move ever nearer to your spirit and purpose in life. We all want to be seen and heard. There is no better time than today. No better way for those of us who have felt silenced than to speak up now through our art. It's time we all die to who we've been. It's time we wake up to who we came here to be.

Forms of Creativity

There are more forms of creativity than there are seconds in a day and drops of water in the sea. For our purposes, we lump all forms under the umbrella of *creativity* and call all those who act on behalf of creative expression *creatives*.

Following are four major types of creativity. Which one or ones are you most likely to use or attract(s) you the most? Identify your relationship to each type and list the projects, inspirations, or daydreams that fall under each one.

Spontaneous Creativity. Spontaneous creativity is intuitive and expresses emotion through images and visions, patterns and colors, words and rhythms from a moment of inspiration. Unstructured art causes others to think and feel. You're moved to replicate the image you saw reflected in a puddle. A color spins a story in your imagination.

List your relationship to *spontaneous creativity* and your projects, inspirations, or daydreams that seemed to come out of nowhere.

_____

_____

_____

_____

Innovative Creativity. Innovative creativity builds on what others have done in new and dynamic ways to revolutionize stagnant constructs, modernize outdated models, and breathe freshness into a stale genre. Tested and accepted images are improved upon. What has become common and ordinary evolves into something new and remarkable.

List your relationship to *innovative creativity* and your projects, inspirations, or daydreams that seemed to come in response to a need for improvement.

_____

_____

_____

_____

Original Creativity. Original creativity applies power and magic to old formulas. Turns the typical upside down. Imagines an ingenious route around entrenched obstacles. Invents something entirely new.

List your relationship to *original creativity* and your projects, inspirations, or daydreams that seemed to come from inside of you.

_____

_____

_____

_____

_____

Deliberate Creativity. Deliberate creativity breaks an artistic pursuit into pieces and forms the parts into a plan of action with a specific beginning, middle, and end. Deliberate creativity as a craft to accomplish a specific artistic activity requires certain skills and serves a tangible purpose.

List your relationship to *deliberate creativity* and your projects, inspirations, or daydreams that arose out of deliberation for a specific purpose.

_____

_____

_____

_____

_____

All forms of creativity offer life-changing opportunities, but deliberate creativity poses a unique set of challenges that creates a great chance for transformation. For that reason, *Boundless Creativity* invites you to explore deliberate creativity through this program. Feel free to incorporate elements from the other forms of creativity too.

DREAMS AND DESIRES

Often, while dealing with everyday dramas and commitments, we daydream about a way out, a plan beyond, a creative solution and change. The following comments were recorded from a group of creatives brainstorming dreams.

"I design jewelry in my imagination and dream of making the pieces real."

"I'd love to turn my young adult novel into a movie script."

"I want to finish the crib before the baby is born."

Here at the beginning of the program, you're asked to dream big as you explore your aspirations for deliberate creativity. Beginnings are times of

- grandiose dreams,

- thoughts of escape,

- desires to change, and

- imagined possibilities.

Beginnings are not the time to think rationally about all the reasons why you shouldn't or couldn't dream and desire what you want. You will be provided plenty of opportunities later in the program to analyze and quantify. For now, simply let your imagination roam free.

Which dreams of yours have come true?

_____

_____

_____

Which of your dreams haven't come true?

_____

_____

_____

Unrealized Dreams

There are countless reasons why your dreams haven't come true or worked out and why your desires remain unrealized. Some are inner reasons. Others are reasons outside of us. You write songs and form a band when you're young with dreams of making it big, but then you get married, have a family, and put your dream aside. Now your children have flown the nest, you have a fulfilling career, and you're eager to resurrect what once was your absorbing passion. In college, a teacher says your drawings will never amount to anything. Once, you believed her. Now, you hope differently. As a kid, you wrote a bunch of three-act plays that you and your siblings performed. You haven't a clue why you stopped writing but are eager to start again. A parent says your dream is ridiculous and tells you to come down out of the clouds and do something productive. Finally, you're ready to see if you were right all along.

Fondest Desires

Now it's your turn. Surrender to your fondest desires.

1. Set a timer for ten minutes. Brainstorm dreams, desires, and goals from long ago—things still stored in your imagination—along with those you entertain now and as you imagine yourself in your later years. Jot down as many as you can as quickly as you can. Include those dreams and goals that represent the completion of a series of external actions toward a creative end (doing what you want). Also include dreams that lead to mastery over a weakness and have something to do with creativity. Add to the list as other ideas pop up.

    _____

    _____

    _____

    _____

    _____

    _____

2. Circle the dreams and goals you can achieve by yourself without help from others. For example:

    • Don't circle *"win the Pulitzer Prize."* Do circle *"finish my novel."*

    • Don't circle *"get an agent."* Do circle *"submit manuscript to agents."*

3. Prioritize, placing the dream or goal that tugs and whispers and invites you the most at number one.

4. Underline those desires or wishes that have to do with spirit, emotions, personality, strengths and weaknesses, and beliefs.

5. Highlight creative dreams with a specific and concrete end you can reach within a definable deadline. These deal with jobs, hobbies, passions, art, and crafts.

Breathe! Remember what you do here is just the beginning. You'll have plenty of time later in the program to deepen your understanding of your outer and inner goals and refine them. Do your best. Write something. Get started…

TAKE ACTION

Today, try one spontaneous act of creativity. Paint. Draw. Write. Sing. Dance. Do it now. Add flair and beauty to something you do. Use your imagination. Refresh something dated. See what is and try something different. After work, take the long, slow, and scenic way home. Make chalk drawings on the sidewalk. Leave rocks you've decorated with inspiring words in random places for others to find. Create a playlist with songs that feed your energy and uplift your spirit. Don't prepare. Don't think. Be spontaneous. Do! Create one new thing. If what you choose to create has something to do with one of your creativity dreams, so much the better.

Record what you create and how you feel as you create.

_____

_____

_____

_____

_____

_____

_____

STEP 2

Opposition to Your Creativity Goals

The Universal Story leads to transformation. Phase 1, Know Yourself, centers around creating an inner spiritual goal and an outer creativity goal to take on your voyage into the Sea of Creativity toward change. We begin with the outer creativity goal.

In step 1, you listed dreams and desires you entertain. Before you choose one to develop, first, let's talk about the opposition you're likely to meet. Anyone who decides to live a creative life faces the daunting task of making choices outside the norm, choices that may upset others.

A creative life requires that we take action. And every action we take creates an equal and opposite reaction. Opposition demands you fight through trials or lose energy and put the goal aside. As long as we give up our personal power to another person or a belief, antagonists will dominate and bully us.

There is another way. You acknowledge what blocks you. You search for the message from the Universal Story about the significance and meaning of the opposition, the obstacle, the setback, the disaster, the bullying, or the foe. Often, the greatest lesson in a conflict is learning how to hold onto your own power while also allowing the other person their personal power too.

When you're confronted with the internal opposition of exhaustion, discouragement, fear, and negativism, how often do you get side-tracked, give up completely, or let whatever opposes you have its way?

Rarely   *Occasionally*   *Frequently*   *Constantly*

When you're confronted with the external opposition of mockery, sarcasm, criticism, and intimidation, how often do you get sidetracked, give up completely, or let whatever or whoever opposes you have their way?

Rarely   *Occasionally*   *Frequently*   *Constantly*

NEW IDEAS THREATEN THE OLD

Creativity arrives with ordeals and hardships. That's what it means to live a creative life—you explore life around you differently than the generally accepted ways of doing things. You try new things. When you use your imagination, your originality represents change and is often met with resistance. New ideas threaten the old and disrupt the balance of power. In addition, your devotion to your creativity often elicits resistance from others.

"Well, you're happy, but now the rest of the family has to fend for ourselves."

"Your time would be better spent getting a real job that pays you."

"You know there's no guarantee you're going to succeed."

Whatever the opposition—internal or external—its primary role is to test your readiness for the next step. Opposition symbolizes sacred turning points in a rite of passage. If your beliefs are too limiting, you struggle. If you keep doing as you always have, you forsake change. If whatever or whoever opposes you wants success more than you do, you abandon your goals. Your attitude about your readiness, as much as anything, determines success.

Are you ready to face whatever opposition comes your way to live a creative life?

Yes   *No*

If you answered no, what must you do to move from being half-hearted and ho-hum to passionate about living your dreams?

_____

_____

_____

_____

_____

A great attitude comes from a willingness to view problems symbolically. Rather than allowing them to produce stress, view everything that stands in your way to success as an opportunity to stretch your imagination, practice a new approach, and adopt new beliefs. As a mom, a father, or a student, and as an artist, writer, or entrepreneur, you're required to come up with creative solutions on the fly. The more often you're challenged, the more agile and inspired you become—a self-confident creative.

In Preparation

The challenges and opposition you meet prepare you for the next step in your spiritual voyage. To succeed, you may need more information than you currently have, more physical strength, more insight, more determination, a valuable trick, or a deeper understanding of what you're doing and why.

If we're not growing and changing, our art suffers. Our spirit shrinks. Then a physical ailment hits. A bum knee, a bad back, sickness turn us immobile. When we're stuck, we're likely overcompensating for bad things we imagine at every turn. In avoiding a dangerous place, project, situation, person, or people, we freeze, hoping not to be spotted. As important as safety is, the pursuit of security is limiting. The greatest expansion involves the greatest risk. Transformation and creativity demand courage and a willingness to learn from whatever comes.

OPPOSITION REPRESENTS WHAT YOU'RE HERE TO LEARN

Do you ever feel like you keep making the same mistakes and often are faced with the exact same dilemma you thought you were finished with? You're excited about an art project you dreamed up and promise yourself that this time you're keeping your plans to yourself. The next thing you know, you're telling your friends and family all about your idea. When you finally show up to take the steps needed, you find you're out of energy and have lost your enthusiasm for the project. You begin writing a poem, work for days, read over what you composed, and crumple it in the trash. You knew she couldn't be trusted and yet you opened up again anyway.

"This same old argument. Really?"

"I'm so sick of wallowing in this pathetic rut."

"Someday I'm going to learn how to open my mouth and say how I feel."

The time you devote to learning from the highs and lows of creativity and life itself reduces the likelihood of meeting that same opposition again—and again—until finally you learn the meaning of the message offered you. Getting knocked down and immediately picking yourself up and trying again is all well and good. However, for growth and change to flourish, a valuable approach is first to accept the misstep, the failure, and the foe as learning experiences. And then, before trying again, pause and absorb the wisdom offered in the opposition.

Types of Opposition

I introduce the reality of opposition inherent in every creative endeavor not to scare you. I want to open your eyes to a new way of living by making friends with the adversity that arises throughout every spiritual life. Opposition is not to be feared or felled by or taken personally but accepted as a valuable part, even the most valuable part, of the voyage itself.

The goal of this program is to ignite your passion to create. Opposition is anything that threatens to douse dreams and interfere or block or constrain growth and transformation. Every creative goal comes with teachings and instructions created especially for you to advance your spiritual development.

What most depletes your energy to create?

_____

_____

_____

_____

_____

Following are two major kinds of opposition you're likely to meet when living your best creative life.

Internal Opposition

As part of my research, I ask writers and creatives to complete a profile with their dreams and opposition. When asked what stands in their way of achieving their goals, the vast majority answers the same way:

"Me!"

And what is their greatest fear? For this, the answers are equally divided:

"Success!"

"Failure!"

The most powerful opposition we face is made up of our own negative thoughts and unproductive habits. Our focus turns to your inner opposition in step 3.

External Opposition

External opposition is any human and nonhuman antagonists that oppose your dreams and goals and actions. Following are a few of the more common sources of opposition creatives face.

Friends, other people, and jobs. Most of us are content living as we're expected and taking steps sanctioned by an authority outside of us. We create a code of ethics based on our patriarchal society, family expectations, and religious dogma, all of which perpetuate the comfort of conformity. We do our best to go after our dreams, though most of us haven't moved as far ahead as we may have hoped. And we keep the peace by not upsetting the usual order of things.

How do you rank yourself?   *Follower*   *Rule breaker*

How important is fitting in to you?   *Very*   *Moderately*   *Not much*

Nature and time. Flooding, wind, drought, heat, and cold direct your attention away from creating. The seasons, the time of the day, and the day of the week can stifle creativity. When surveyed for major obstructions to creativity, creatives often mention time.

"*I have too much time on my hands and end up squandering it.*"

"*Too many demands on my time.*"

"*I have trouble taking time away from work and my family to finish.*"

How do you rank your relationship with time?

Never enough   *Too much*   *Somewhere in between*

Our personal environment. You've braved the rocks and survived the rapids, and you suddenly discover you're in the heart of creativity. An almost out-of-body experience and with joyful abandon, you bloom; you become a channel, a mouthpiece, an instrument and agent for creativity to reveal more of what's on the other side of the veil. An image emerges on canvas. Words flow across the page.

In our haste to keep up with our imagination, our environment often turns messy—dishes left undone, beds unmade, papers strewn everywhere, sawdust in your hair, and even wood chips in your bed. Optimum is having a dedicated space where you can leave your work and then jump right back into it when so moved. If you leave out what you're working on, aware of the next step you plan to take, you slip right back into your bliss.

Messiness is a universally recognized trait of creatives. Messiness becomes an antagonist if it constricts your imagination and causes the free flow of creative energy to evade you. Begin a habit of organizing and purging and cleansing your space before beginning a new project and at each major turning point.

How do you rank yourself in terms of organization?

Organized   *Disorganized*   *Somewhere in between*

Watch for Sharks

In this section, you're asked to identify likely opposition you'll face. Again, leave your own fears and flaws off your list for now. In other words, even if you feel that some of your own inner beliefs or traits or habits interfere with you reaching your goals, for now, let those go. Continue to concentrate on external opposition.

List external oppositions you've faced in your life. Review your list of dreams and desires. Antagonists stare back at you.

_____

_____

_____

_____

_____

Next, list external antagonists or potential antagonists in your life right now who may have something to say about this program and what you're doing. Especially as you grow and change, who may object? Include anyone or anything or any place that depletes your energy, enthusiasm, and excitement.

_____

_____

_____

_____

_____

Beginning Today

Become hypervigilant about how you feel in environments you frequent, with people you're usually in contact with, and at certain times of the day and night. Learn how to spot antagonists—those people, places, or things that set you back, deaden your energy, interfere with your progress, demean your efforts, ignore you, or disrespect you.

Where and when and with whom do you feel the safest and the most supported to be completely yourself?

_____

_____

_____

_____

_____

_____

Where and when and with whom do you feel uninspired, lethargic, and least supported to be completely yourself?

_____

_____

_____

_____

_____

_____

Some antagonists you can reason with or change. Others are best to be avoided, at least for now. Remember, we're not going to shy away from adversity or turn our backs on challenges. But until you have a better grasp of the meaning they bring to your life, for now its best if you avoid people, places, and things that block you.

TAKE ACTION

In preparation for your voyage into the Sea of Creativity, begin purging and cleaning your environment. Start small with a drawer, a closet, your desk, the guest room, or the garage. Share what you no longer treasure. Let go of all possessions but those you cherish. Donate old clothes. Fix leaky faucets. Scrub the floor. Shake a rattle to awaken old stale energy. Fling open the windows. And as you do, flick your fingers to direct the energy out while chanting, "Be gone. Be gone. Be gone." Think of these actions as steps in a cleansing ritual of letting go of what's no longer needed as you make room in your life to pursue a lofty goal.

Internal Opposition and Strengths

Our creativity originates on the other side of a veil, in a place where dreams and our spirit live. We inhabit the mundane side of the veil with our mind patterns, emotions, personality traits, and limited beliefs, each of which contributes to self-doubt, emotional traps, and the other creative blocks that form the basis of this workbook.

In our daydreams, we come across as committed and energetic. In real life, however, our best self is often missing, underdeveloped, or hiding beneath convention, damaging habits, and prejudices that interfere with achieving creative success.

In step 2, you identified external opposition in the form of people, places, and anything with the potential to interfere with you reaching your creativity dreams. Now we travel inward to assess how your personality traits and habits both support and interfere with your creativity.

PERSONALITY TRAITS

The stronger your personality grows, the more fixed the veil and distant your spirit are. Your spirit is your essence, core, aliveness, and inner wisdom. Your personality forms as layers around your spirit as you navigate the material world. The difference between your personality traits and spiritual wisdom is that spirit is unchanging and eternal. Your personality, however, can be transformed to once again honor your intuition, your knowing, and your heart with the help of insight, discipline, and experience.

We attract people and events into our lives through our personality traits and quirks, but we also turn others away. The shadow side of our personality develops when our traits keep us from what we want in life. Wandering in darkness, our spirit and creative energy fade.

Examples of Personality Traits

The personality traits in italics are examples of characteristics that could keep you from living a successful creative life. (Not every line in the list below will have something italicized.)

Organized versus Messy

Curious versus *Cautious*

Assertive versus *Passive*

Outgoing versus Solitary

Stable and Calm versus Spontaneous
and excitable

Energetic versus *Lethargic*

Suspicious versus Compassionate

Cooperative versus *Antagonistic*

Indecisive versus Confident

Optimist versus *Pessimist*

Competitive versus Helpful

Inventive versus *Consistent*

Perfectionist versus Realist

Efficient versus Easy-going

Enthusiastic versus *Reserved*

Nervous versus Confident

Open versus *Shut down*

Original versus *Traditional*

Procrastination versus Proactive

Identify and honestly assess the positive personality traits you consider your strengths.

_____

_____

_____

_____

_____

_____

_____

Identify and honestly assess the negative personality traits with the potential to stifle your creativity and that may prove detrimental to living your best creative life. Some traits can be both dark and light. For example, being ambitious can be both a flaw and a strength.

List negative traits from most prominent to least obvious.

_____

_____

_____

_____

_____

_____

PERSONALITY AND MIND HABITS

Our habits, both physical and mind habits, affect the flourishing or withering of our creativity. A personality habit is a settled practice and your typical manner of behavior in a given situation. Your habit may be to work from morning till night. You may have a tendency to gossip or to sleep in front of the television. You're a worrywart. You're always finishing other people's sentences. After work, you like to fix a drink and have a smoke.

Mind habits are your usual manner of thinking. They pattern our reactions to life in predicable ways and create our reality.

"It never ends up looking like I imagined."

"If I don't do it myself, it won't get done right."

"What's the point?"

Habits are formed by our beliefs and lessons learned, often during times of intense emotions. What we believe creates what will be; it drives our current behavior.

Anything you do regularly and often—sometimes without knowing you're doing it or why—is a routine, a pattern and an established custom, and it is hard to give up. A habit becomes an addiction when we repeatedly or compulsively involve ourselves in a dependency, even knowing how detrimental it is to our spirit and despite the harmful consequences we know we'll suffer.

Examples of Personality and Mind Habits

Italicized personality and mind habits are examples of patterns that could keep you from living a successful creative life. (Not every line in the list below will have something italicized.)

Daydreamer versus Doer

Alert versus *Asleep*

Aware of prime creative time versus *Oblivious to personal productive time of the day or night*

Spends quiet alone time versus *Busy with family and friends and activities*

Stick-to-itiveness versus *Gives up easily*

Lazy versus Self-starter

Sticks with what works versus Tries new things

Takes risks versus *Doing things as they always been done*

Seeks opportunities for self-expression everyday versus *Ignores personal needs, desires, and uniqueness*

Acts from a desire for recognition or an external prize versus Acts from an internal desire

Enjoys shaking things up versus *Enjoys things to stay the same*

Thrives on a set routine versus Spontaneous

Gossips versus Stays quiet and keeps to yourself

Excessive drinking versus Moderation

Takes something to sleep at night versus Keeps your sleeping mind clear

Chooses bullies versus Attracts supportive people

Looks on the bright side versus *Convinced of the dark side*

Suppresses feelings to keep peace with others versus Honest attempts to open up

Identify and honestly assess your personality and mental habits that have the potential to stifle your creativity and that may prove detrimental to living your best creative life. Some patterns can be both dark and light. For example, a habit of shaking things up stimulates creativity while it can also arouse confusion. Rank your negative habits from most prominent to least obvious.

_____

_____

_____

_____

_____

Personality Traits and Habits as They Support Creativity

Now evaluate your personality traits and habits that support your dreams and goals. Nurture and strengthen any personality traits and habits you discover that speed you toward your creative goals. For example, your habit of daydreaming inspires a new idea or provides a solution to a challenge. A self-starter, you set out to create every day at the same time. Your habit of taking a daily walk by the shore opens time and space to let your mind wander and rest.

When asked about his strengths, one creative answered:

"Endurance, and I refuse to give up."

His personality traits have the potential to override a bad habit and ensure that he'll reach whatever he chooses for an external goal.

Identify and honestly assess your personality traits and habits that may prove helpful in living your best creative life. Rank positive traits and habits from most prominent to least obvious.

_____

_____

_____

_____

_____

PERSONALITY TRAITS AND HABITS AS INTERNAL OPPOSITION

You faced certain unpleasant aspects of how you either knowingly or unknowingly sabotage yourself. In the previous example, struggle ensues when the determined creative also has a negative trait or dark habit that challenges his strengths.

"If I don't drink my self to death in the process."

Personality habits and traits can be antagonists, depending on you and the way in which you use the traits. Though it's usually vastly easier to identify positive traits than to face our flaws, the personality traits we're most interested in identifying are shortcomings, weaknesses, inadequacies, faults, or limiting beliefs. Personality flaws, prejudices, fears, and really any imperfection that mars and blocks the way to your creativity goals are deadly internal antagonists that will challenge your greatness.

A vital part of living a creative life is the confidence to embrace your inner strength and belief in yourself. This means that any personality traits and habits that tries to sabotage you must be modified, changed, or eliminated. As you may suspect, the following trait immediately shuts down the creative experience.

"It's difficult for me to allow for any initial imperfections."

The creative who said this will never achieve her creativity goals until she learns to embrace imperfection, accept those unformed buds of possibility as they present themselves, and view everything as perfect in its own way.

Another creative intends to create a masterpiece while also carrying the belief that she isn't good enough, smart enough, or rich or poor enough. Something in the mix has to change. Settle for less in your external expectations and relationships and life. Or identify and overcome your internal antagonists, change your perception of your self-worth, and learn to value what you have.

What internal beliefs most limit you?

_____

_____

_____

_____

_____

Flaws

To live your best creative life, you're well served if you can let the creative energy flow. Any belief or trait or habit that blocks energy is a flaw.

"I lack discipline."

"I'm stubborn and insist on doing things my way."

"I give up easily."

Flaws develop in your personality over time. To be loved and accepted, we do lots of compromising. Fade our light so others can shine. Take care of others' needs before our own. Don't question or argue, get along and smile. All of this leads to living everyone else's life and leaving yours an unlived life.

Flawed thinking, beliefs, traits, and habits interfere with you being who you wish to be, getting what you desire in life, maintaining healthy relationships, and inspiring your imagination and dreams. But this internal opposition is self-created and can be eliminated. One creative voiced her flaws:

"Evil voices in my head, procrastination, a lack of time, procrastination, and the ever-popular fear of failure or success."

You considered your dreams in step 1, both past dreams and things you want to strive for now. Of the goals you attempted but never achieved or that simply died, which ones faded because your flaws got in the way?

_____

_____

_____

_____

_____

Flaws are acquired from life experiences—both dark and light experiences. Superstitious habits develop around both successes and flawed thinking as safeguards against future failures. You have what you perceive as a negative experience. You relive the events in your mind. You think about what happened. You form judgments about the events and other people's behavior and your own actions. Decisions you make based on those stories shape your goals.

You make a bad decision and lose your confidence. You begin letting others influence your decisions because you're afraid to trust yourself. You're a perfectionist and afraid to begin because you know you'll fail. You did horribly in school, which forms a belief of not being smart enough to live the life of your dreams. Give in to these limiting stories, and you settle for a mediocre existence devoid of creativity and never fully actualize your promise.

Write about an experience, while not the most extreme and perhaps a bit mundane, that went sour because of your flaw?

_____

_____

_____

_____

_____

_____

See into Your Own Heart

When asked what was stopping her, one creative answered, "Any excuse will do."

Sometimes it's hard to see into our own hearts. We know what other people's flaws are, how they hold themselves back. We even conjecture why they do what they do. We have trouble doing the same for ourselves, partly because our egos refuse to confront our weaknesses—but mostly because we're afraid of what we'll find.

"Until recently, I blamed family members who seemed to block my creative efforts. Now it's more than that. To paraphrase Snoopy, I have met the enemy, and it is me—and my failure to assert my right to create."

What would your family or friends say is your greatest flaw?

_____

_____

_____

Are they right?   Yes   No

As you answer the questions throughout this workbook, find a quiet space and take your time. Meditate on the exercises. Ask for help. When a trusted friend tells you how they believe you hold yourself back, no matter how badly you want to jump in and defend yourself, be open and grateful. Remember, whatever they say about you first travels through their own ego and flaws and may have everything to do with them and absolutely nothing at all to do with you.

TAKE ACTION

Experiment with five (or more) forms of creativity you're attracted to—weaving, writing, painting murals, gardening, forging metal art, working with stained glass, blowing glass, printmaking, filming a movie, making ceramics. The list is endless. Think differently. Problem solve in new and unexpected ways. Write a song. Add your own flair to an old recipe. Explore how you feel designing a shirt with pen and ink, drawing a self-portrait with crayons, laying a lovely table for breakfast, lunch, and dinner for one or many, making candles, and crafting soap.

"What a mess."

"I can't explain it, but at one point when I was completely engrossed in what I was doing, I felt this joy and sense of free flow."

"I can't believe I actually created something with my own two hands!"

Circle your energy level during and after trying the creative projects you're drawn to explore.

Energy level during creativity: *Low*   *Average*   *High*

Energy level immediately after creativity: *Low*   *Average*   *High*

STEP 4

Dreams into Reality

We're nearly at the end of phase 1 of the Universal Story. Time to pack the two most important items before embarking on the odyssey. The work you do now is a starting point for comparison as you progress through the four phases of living your best creative life.

With your perceived inner and outer opposition in mind, explore your outer artistic ambitions. One of your dreams and desires will decide both your external creativity goal and your internal spiritual goal. The outer creative goal determines your course of action. Your spiritual goal reflects your inner emotional life and forms the direction of your personal transformation. For the first half of this step, we focus on a creativity goal that requires action. Your tandem inner spiritual goal comes later.

OUTER CREATIVE GOAL

A dream is ethereal and imbued with forces conspiring to grant us our desires. Deliberate creativity goals formed around a dream are outer goals. They're desires with a plotted plan of action. When one creative was asked what her goals were for herself now that her kids were leaving for college, she kept mentioning goals she had for her children. Each time, I gently led her back to herself and her own goals, but she just couldn't seem to remember what she had dreamed for herself.

Choose a dream, desire, or goal from the list you created in step 1. Or, better yet, choose something entirely new that recently burst forth. The ideal is a creative desire that excites you and even sets off a flutter of butterflies in your stomach.

"I dream of being an interior designer."

"I want to illustrate picture books."

"My secret desire is to live by the sea."

Of the dreams and desires that inspire you, pick one.

_____

_____

Next, select a creativity milestone that supports your vision and is relevant to reaching your chosen dream. A secret desire to live by sea involves energy markers, milestones, and giant steps. A dream more complex and challenging than you're capable of achieving all at once is best split into a sequence of smaller steps and actions.

"I snap pictures at the coast, share them, and declare my dream on social media."

"I write a poem about my life living at the sea and submit it to a poetry contest."

"I paint an ombré effect on my bedroom wall of the sky and sea blending as one."

Defined goals like these form an external creativity goal. For this time through the program, start with something manageable.

Divide your chosen dream into the major steps and actions needed to achieve your goal. (Don't worry if you don't know all the necessary steps now. You'll have time later as you learn more about your chosen field of endeavor to fill in what's missing.)

_____

_____

_____

_____

_____

_____

_____

Three Key Elements

Outer creativity goals focus your actions on completing specific tasks for each forward step. Whether passionate about expressing your creativity through song, drama, weaving, dance, painting, writing, sculpting, filmmaking, fashion design, scrap-booking, writing a musical, animating a webinar, designing your website, or decorating your studio, conjure up just one goal that involves creativity with a sequence of steps you can manage on your own and you're willing to commit to.

Using the first action part of the dream you choose to pursue, incorporate the following three key elements to create your external creativity goal: use a positive and present tense, have a clear deadline, and make your goal measurable.

POSITIVE AND PRESENT TENSE

The following creativity goals are positive and written in the present tense, as if they've been reached and are already true.

"I design and construct a signature arm cuff as the first step toward fulfilling my dream of creating my own jewelry line."

"I design an avant-garde jumpsuit, sew it, and post a picture of me wearing it on social media."

"I paint five still-life oil paintings on canvas, and, whether I like them or not, I post each one on Instagram."

Imagine that time is nonlinear (not real) and that your goal is realized. Seeing your goal written in a positive, present tense clears the way for you to catch up to what is already real. Rather than write a goal about what you don't want to do anymore, won't do, shouldn't do, or are going to stop doing, instead, write what you will do in its place.

Write a goal that involves several steps in present tense and the positive.

_____

_____

_____

_____

A DEADLINE

Deadlines get a bad rap. Just read the word "deadline," and palms start to sweat. Resistance kicks in. But as with all things, there is a light side to deadlines. Have you ever noticed that on nights when you're firm about when you wish to wake up, you invariably awaken in the morning at that precise time?

The deadline you give yourself to complete your creativity goal functions in much the same way. When we commit to completing something by a precise date, our body, mind, and spirit collude to give us what we want. Celebrate if you reach your deadline successfully. Then craft your next creativity goal.

And if you don't reach your deadline? Simply acknowledge that you have something more to learn. However, if we mean to succeed by such-and-such a date, we often do.

What is your experience with deadlines?

Good   *Bad*   *Indifferent*   *No experience with deadlines*

Estimate the time it will take you to finish the exercises in the workbook and preform the necessary tasks to reach your goal. Decide on a realistic time frame, one you'll actually stick to. For now, one month to complete your goal gives you time to get in the rhythm of showing up daily for your creativity. In fact, depending on the speed in which you act, your strengths, and with only slight opposition, each of the examples above is reachable in a month. If, however, you're apt to wait until the last minute, until the sense of urgency drives you, tighten your deadline to squeeze all the empty air out of the equation.

"I film a short in the next three weeks."

"I produce an art show by the gallery's assigned deadline."

"I make a music video, write the rough draft of a story, construct a website, generate a social media presence, or manufacture a video game by _____."

The shorter the time frame here in the beginning, the more manageable the task. Center yourself with full acceptance of where you are right now. Be realistic in deciding what you can achieve and in what amount of time.

Now rewrite your creativity goal in the present tense, in a positive way, and include a deadline.

_____

_____

_____

_____

_____

_____

MEASUREABLE

The next essential element for your creativity goal is how progress is measured. External change comes as you make your way to your creative goal. With each step you take—a precise word count per day, the amount of time spent creating, or the total number of steps necessary for completion and how many were accomplished—you live a creative life. In the end, you hold the physical manifestation of a dream or desire.

To stay on track, decide how you'll measure your progress. If it is too vague and missing a tangible outcome, neither you nor your supportive forces will be clear about what you want and where you're headed. Instead, offer details about what you'll see, hear, feel, and touch—in other words, tangible evidence of the goal's end result while successfully meeting your deadline. That way, you'll be able to track success and anticipate new accomplishments and rewards as you push yourself forward with excitement.

Now rewrite your creativity goal with a deadline and what you define as achieving your external creativity goal.

_____

_____

_____

_____

_____

What Calls Your Name

Practice writing positive goals in the present tense with a deadline and end result. Begin with creativity goals that are within your reach. Don't be too serious or focus on goals you think you *should* pursue or *ought* to do or that everyone else is doing. (If you've learned to rely on others for permission to make your own decisions, this may be challenging.)

Lean in to what calls your name and excites you. Lean in to what scares you because it's just not done or people won't like it or you'll lose your position in the community and the respect of friends and family. Focus instead on what you'll gain, and do it anyway.

Generate as many goals that enliven you to begin as you can come up with. This way, you create a fun creative life. Creativity thrives in a vibrant and hopeful spirit.

Write your list of goals here.

_____

_____

_____

_____

_____

_____

_____

_____

_____

_____

Choose one outer creativity goal you're ready to commit to. Write a measurable goal in present tense, using action verbs and a positive tone. Include a deadline and how you will know you've succeeded at achieving the goal. This is your outer creativity goal.

_____

_____

_____

_____

INNER SPIRITUAL GOAL

As wonderful as it is to hold a tangible piece of art that you created in your hands, the even greater gift lies in the inner changes and transformation you go through on your way to success.

Spiritual goals are inner goals you decide to address to live your best creative life. Spiritual dreams are visions of your perfect self—sure-footed and confident in your perfect environment. In your spiritual daydreams, you come across joyful and creative, even if in real life, you're often sad and apt to beat yourself up.

Evaluate your strengths and weaknesses in relationship to the creativity dreams you're adopting for your work here. These visions point to inner aspects you strive for while simultaneously moving toward your creative goals. Close your eyes and imagine your actions and feelings as you live your best creative life.

List any current traits and beliefs or habits you display now that you'd prefer to discard.

_____

_____

_____

_____

_____

List the traits and beliefs and habits you consider strengths that you're proud to take forward with you.

_____

_____

_____

_____

_____

_____

_____

Move Inward

Spiritual dreams are made up of two types of energy. Light energy is symbolic of a joyful and spiritual drive. Dark energy reflects fearful powerlessness and sorrowful withdrawal. Say that you daydream about rapping your poems at a poetry slam. You set a measureable outer goal to recite your poetry in front of other people one month from today. In that daydream, you see the best outcome—people applaud, and you're asked back (light energy). At the same time, doubts and fears (dark energy) creep in. You set an internal dark goal of overcoming fear paired with a light goal of acting with confidence on stage in front of judges.

"I acknowledge my fear and override it with a sense of confidence in myself."

Remember: though that spiritual goal is written as if you're already there, in truth, you'll chant the words countless times to rewire your mind habits and emotions.

By forming a spiritual goal out of the dark energy, I don't mean goals that can harm you, others, or the environment. I mean using personality traits you're ashamed of or frustrated by or oblivious to. On the flip side of whatever dark or shadow traits you possess, there are opposite and equal light habits, beliefs, and traits. Your spiritual goal incorporates both a dark and light aspect of your personality. By strengthening one helpful trait while extinguishing a destructive trait, you create an overall inner spiritual goal that improves the quality of your life and that of those around you.

Some habits and beliefs run deeper than others. Don't start with your most stuck pattern. And be aware that you may not even consciously know when you fall into your confusion, desire revenge, blame, deny your own needs, block your good, or let others decide, or when you're nursing old hurts, holding too tightly, and denying most vehemently.

What is your most stuck pattern?

_____

_____

_____

_____

_____

When the time comes for you to begin the steps to achieving your creativity goal, you will become aware each time you react judgmentally about what you're creating. You admit the day you wasted procrastinating wasn't because of whatever external thing you blamed—it was because of you yourself. You begin practicing compassion for others and for yourself. This way, when you achieve your creative goal of winning first prize in a short story contest, performing an intuitive dance on stage, or designing and crafting shoes, you've also changed how you act and react, as well as your beliefs about yourself and others.

Two-Part Inner Goal

Creativity involves the coming together of traits, habits, emotions, and behaviors. It involves eliminating unhelpful "shadow" traits and strengthening "light" traits.

SHADOW

A multitude of flaws, beliefs, attitudes, dark traits, or shadow habits stifle creativity, prevent access to inspiration, turn you lethargic and uninspired, or kill your creative dreams. Consider your outer creativity goal, and then choose the shadow trait or habit most likely to trip you up as you pursue that goal.

"At night, instead of imagining the next step in my creativity project, my mind twists and turns, worrying about all sorts of unrelated things I can't really do anything about, but still I worry. By morning I'm exhausted and uninspired."

"I'm impatient and grow frustrated by the discipline and time it takes to achieve my goal, and then I don't do it."

"I'm easily distracted and prone to procrastination."

You may be intimately familiar with one or several of the following flaws, beliefs, attitudes, dark traits, or shadow habits: fear, frustration, perfectionism, procrastination, impatience, self-doubt, self-trivializing, giving up, self-rejection, resistant, insecurity, controlling, withholding, resentment, anxiety, and guilt. Likely you have your own brand of fiendish internal opposition. Pick the demon you're most likely to meet as you go after your creativity goal.

Choose a shadow trait, belief, or habit to focus on and overcome for your inner spiritual goal. Write it down.

_____

_____

_____

LIGHT

On the flip side of whatever shadow traits you possess, there are opposite and equal light traits that support your creativity. Survey the personality traits and habits you brainstormed in step 3. Look for habits you've developed that feed your energy to create. Resilience, resourcefulness, patience, appreciation, devotion, gratitude, trust, acceptance, encouragement, self-confidence, passion, and forgiveness are examples of light traits developed over time that buoy your creative dreams and allow your spirit to soar.

"I believe in myself."

"I focus on what I'm grateful for."

"I'm a hard worker, and I love solving puzzles."

Choose one skill, ability, trait, habit, belief, or other kind of strength to feature as you move into the middle of the program to higher creativity. Pick the one that best supports the outer creativity goal you've chosen and best serves you in reaching it.

Write it down here.

_____

_____

_____

AFFIRMATION

An affirmation—a pledge, mantra, or chant—repeated often and with meaning, connects your spirit to miraculous support in reaching your dreams. By turning your inner spiritual goal into an affirmation, you have what you need to reprogram your brain in a way that best serves your creativity. Whatever you choose to call it, the mantra you'll use both acknowledges one of your weaknesses and applauds one of your strengths.

"I override my doubts about my ability to accomplish my creativity goal by celebrating and giving thanks for my determination to get me here."

"I watch for early signs of being overwhelmed and self-doubt so I can step in with my skill of rising above limitations."

"When my fears threaten to turn me apathetic and sluggish, my imagination and belief in the miraculous stoke the fire inside."

Note how these mantras are stated in present tense, as if already true. Also, they each declare a shadow side of the person's nature as well as a positive side. The first step in extinguishing one habit and strengthen another is to become acutely aware of your propensity for using one and ignoring the other, respectively. Self-doubt transforms into self-belief. In time and with practice, your light dissolves the shadow.

Combine the flaw you wrote down above with your personal strength, belief, ability, or skill to create a spiritual affirmation and mantra in the present tense. This is your inner spiritual goal.

_____

_____

_____

_____

_____

_____

_____

TAKE ACTION

- Post your refined outer creativity goal and your inner spiritual goal everywhere as reminders of what you're doing and what you believe. You're embarking on a creative project. Only your imagination and strengths are invited along as they take control of your actions back from your weakness.

    - Flash the goal and affirmation across your computer screen.

    - Stick reminders on your bathroom mirror.

    - Put them on your bicycle and in your car.

- Jot both goals on your calendar and block out time for your creativity.

- Final purging: Donate. Recycle. Toss anything old and outdated and that doesn't reflect your creativity goals. Visualize making room for your heart, passion, and life work.

STEP 5

Separation

THE UNIVERSAL STORY

NO TURNING BACK

Know
Yourself

Sea of
Creativity

The energy of the Universal Story in the beginning has awakened slowly, which is quite different to what lies ahead in the middle and even more dramatically at the end. Leave the comfort of your known world and embrace the mystery and possibilities that await you in the Sea of Creativity. Beginnings are meant to be ephemeral. One moment they shine. The next they die.

We all have heaps of dreams and desires we haven't acted on because going back over what's already been lived is passively hypnotic, whereas creating something entirely new involves risks.

"I might embarrass myself."

"I'm too old (or too young, too short, too tall)."

"What will my family say?"

"I could fail."

Well aware of all that has changed during his lifetime and all the changes on the horizon, a grandfather dreams of writing his memoirs for his grandchildren. He thinks about what he wants to write, talks about it, researches, organizes, and keeps explaining to others, though mostly to himself, why he hasn't actually started writing.

Go beyond your usual habit of telling yourself you can always quit whenever you want to. Break from the familiar stories you tell yourself. For the program to work and transformation to occur, commit to it, no matter how uncomfortable, how stuck and balled up you become in search of your own unique creativity and beauty. Until you take action, you haven't moved out of the beginning.

Are you ready to separate from where you currently stand to embark on a voyage into the Sea of Creativity?

Yes   No

LEAVING ONE REALITY FOR ANOTHER

Clutching your outer creativity goal and inner spiritual mantra—both of which define your itinerary—you wait on the dock to embark on your journey. Like a mirage spread out before you, the glittery Sea of Creativity fades and then reappears and comes into view. A tropical breeze blows against your face. The tang of salt water kisses your lips. With screeching gulls overhead, lost in the sound of surf, all your cares float away.

You stand at a threshold. Thresholds signal a heads up. Cross this line, and you leave your old reality. Step forward, and your life shifts. Something new begins. The ritual of letting go of the old, crossing a threshold, and launching into the unknown is a time of separation. You separate from who you've always been and move toward who you're becoming as you actively pursue your creativity goal.

You may believe that you're prepared, that you have a vague sense of the challenges ahead, though nothing can truly ready you for what's coming. Right now, here at the end of the beginning, you're gung-ho, excited, and even passionate. You're in control, working at your own pace, completing the exercises and taking action—and being in control at the beginning sounds far superior to being out of control in the middle and the end, where you have to dive deeply into emotions.

Before you cross the threshold into the mysterious and transcendent Sea of Creativity, first prepare a ritual with symbolism that marks what the crossing means to you.

Rite of Passage

Ancient traditions involve rites of passage to symbolize sacred turning points when the old dies and the new begins.

1. List what you're leaving behind.

_____

_____

_____

2. Create a threshold in nature or simply use the doorway into your workspace, studio, or office.

3. On one side of the threshold, draw whatever most symbolizes your reality now and anything you've decided to leave behind.

4. On the other side of the threshold, create a sign that represents what you're crossing into—your hopes and dreams, the art project you're ready to begin, your spiritual pledge, and perhaps plenty of question marks.

5. Stand on the side of your present reality and what you're leaving behind. Close your eyes. Breathe. Review all you've learned about yourself from the work you've accomplished here in phase 1, "Know Yourself." Make your next breath deep and cleansing.

6. Imagine floating on the Sea of Creativity as the old dissolves into nothing.

7. See yourself taking action toward your creativity goal.

8. Chant your affirmation.

9. Listen to your heart as it beats to the rhythm of the Universal Story.

TAKE ACTION

Take another deep cleansing breath. Now open your eyes. Breathe. Step across the threshold. And as you do, know that there is no turning back…

PHASE 2

The Sea of Creativity

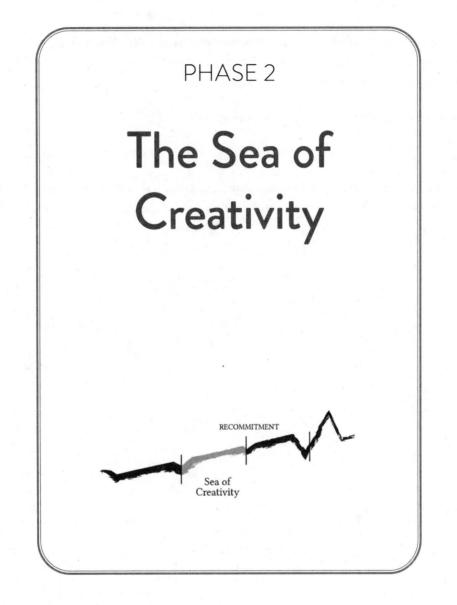

Welcome aboard! In phase 1, you packed for a voyage into sacred waters. Water has long been associated with dreams and emotions, and it symbolizes new dimensions. The Sea of Creativity awakens depths of inspiration to create and grants you access to your spirit.

How do you feel about what you imagine comes next?

Apprehensive   *Excited*   *Something else:* _____

Whether eager or nervous, heady times are ahead as you begin to actively pursue your creativity goal, learn how your emotions affect your energy and creativity, and change the way you interact with yourself and the world around you.

STEP 6

Energy and Emotion

Ready to pursue a lofty goal, create moments of beauty, or follow a dream, you sail the exotic waters of the Sea of Creativity with two goals. Your outer creativity goal defines action steps you plan to take toward your creativity. Your inner spiritual goal defines the emotional and energetic qualities of those actions. Good fortune shines on you as you wrap your life around your creativity.

Take a moment to record your long-term goals again. Include your deadline and measure of success.

Outer Creativity Goal _____

_____

Inner Spiritual Goal _____

_____

Best-case scenario is when your outer creativity goal and inner spiritual goal excite you so much that you've already begun imagining how you'll feel living your best creative life. Perhaps you've jumped in and started taking steps toward your creative goal and are daily chanting your spiritual pledge.

If, however, you had to look back at step 5 to remember what you wrote for your goals, take a moment to evaluate why.

_____

_____

_____

_____

_____

CONFIRM YOUR GOALS

If you're unhappy or unsure or uninspired by your choice of a long-term creativity goal, change it now. Soon you'll be asked to commit to pursuing it all the way to the end.

Likewise, if, after careful thought, the deadline feels unrealistic, adjust it. You're asked to choose a tight deadline for the very reason of breaking down and burning off thoughts and beliefs and blockages that lead to stagnation. At the same time, this program is designed to set you up for success. So think carefully about what you can reasonably achieve in a month.

If you are revising your long-term external creativity goal, write the new version here, in the present tense, as if it's happening right now, with a deadline and a measure of success.

_____

_____

_____

_____

In the same way, if your spiritual pledge is too long to remember, modify it. Keep your pledge brief so it's easy to remember and, like a mantra, rolls off your tongue smoothly. If what you're using now doesn't do much to inspire you to create, build energetic joy, and connect you with your light, ask yourself what mind habit or belief you wish to eliminate to bring power and energy back to yourself. Use that.

"I let go of the past and stand in my highest good."

"Switching my limiting core beliefs about not being worthy to positive personal power excites me."

If necessary, revise your long-term internal spiritual goal.

_____

_____

_____

_____

PLOT THE MYSTERY

Now comes time to adjust your outer and inner realities to fit the way you wish your life to look and function. For that, we turn to the energetic structure beneath all of our lives—the Universal Story.

With the help of the Universal Story, you're asked to plot a suitable plan that works for your individual lifestyle, habits, and strengths. If you're likely to adopt an intensely personal and intuitive approach, keep your plan loose. As you work toward your goals, your creativity is apt to speak to you on its own terms, which means you're best served to be as flexible as possible.

Rather than wander with your head in the clouds, goal setting pulls your dreams into reality by acting on them. We begin with your outer creativity goal.

Short-Term Goals

Creative goals are divided into short-term and long-term goals. Short-term goals are the action steps you believe will advance you to your long-term goal at the end. Measureable and quantifiable goals under your control provide the beginning, middle, and final steps to achieve your goal.

Creatives I meet at conferences often report frustration that they never seem to reach their goals. The problem and the solution revolve around one concrete and tangible element—every creative needs a plan that emboldens you to action. Such a plan involves defining a long-term, measureable goal with a deadline that you will complete. Likely even more important are the short-term goals or steps to get there on time.

Short-term goals give definition to your day-to-day life. For example, if you're an experienced artist determined to paint your daughter's portrait in a month, your action steps revolve around showing up to paint. If, however, you're taking on a new medium, such as learning to watercolor, some of your early steps may include purchasing a book about watercolor painting; searching YouTube for tutorials; purchasing the necessary paper, paints, and brushes; exploring tools and techniques; trying out new ideas; attending classes; and practicing.

With your long-term creativity goal in mind, analyze what steps you plan to take and explore any special factors required for your particular creativity goal. For instance, you dream of performing one of your songs and are too shy to get up in front of people. Your steps may include writing the song, performing it in front of the mirror, then in front of a couple of trusted friends, and next on a sidewalk with people walking by.

Break down your end goal into steps. Arrange those steps in the order needed to achieve your goal. (Don't worry if you don't know all the required steps. We'll deal with that later.)

1. List actions or steps you believe necessary to achieve your creativity goal. Attempt to list these steps in order sequentially. Star those steps you're confident of and excited by.

    _____

    _____

    _____

    _____

    _____

    _____

    _____

    _____

    _____

    _____

    _____

2. Divide the total number of steps you list by three. Mark these steps into three separate and equal sections.

3. Indicate how many days or hours per week you're willing to commit to working on your creativity project in order to meet your deadline. It's great if you plan to show up every day, though this isn't always realistic. Include your start date and deadline date.

    _____

    _____

    _____

As you sail into the mystery, the short-term goals and steps you list make up your itinerary of stopping off places to create.

SKETCH YOUR UNIVERSAL STORY

THE UNIVERSAL STORY

Join me topside with your easel and paint brushes. Use paints or colored pens to draw the foundation of your creativity plan—the Universal Story. Have fun with the activity. Let your creativity loose. Yes, the line itself is linear and static but everything you add to the Universal Story can be as colorful and whimsical as you like.

Creativity is messy. By thinking ahead about the steps you plan to take and plotting them on the Universal Story, you end up with a guide. With the big picture of where you're headed on your creative journey, you can then involve yourself in the day-to-day activities of living your best creative life. A map keeps you centered and grounded as your creativity space becomes cluttered and disorganized.

Let's get started.

☐ Draw a line that looks like the example. Note that the line of the Universal Story rises steadily to illustrate how the energy builds in intensity the further you travel. It's best if you draw the Universal Story line on banner paper you can affix to the wall. That way, you'll see it during the day. This is where you organize and track the steps you plan to take to achieve your creativity goal.

☐ Begin your Universal Story line near the bottom left corner of the paper and draw a solid line that travels steadily upward to a peak about three-quarters of the way across the paper, then drops down into a valley, quickly ascends to an even higher peak, and ends near the right top edge of the paper in a short, falling line.

☐ Add three vertical lines that divide the Universal Story into quarters. In other words, draw a vertical line that ends the first quarter of the Universal Story. Place another line at the halfway point. And draw the third line at the three-quarters mark or after the point where the Universal Story line rises to a peak only to plummet to the lowest point.

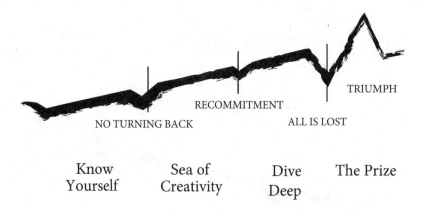

☐ Next, include the name of each phase that corresponds to the section of the Universal Story— Know Yourself, Sea of Creativity, Dive Deep, and The Prize. Also include the name of each major turning point in the same way as you see in the example—No Turning Back, Recommitment, All Is Lost, and Triumph.

Now, hang your map in a place where you will pass it several times a day.

Above the Line

The short-term goals and steps you plan to take toward your long-term creativity goal belong above the Universal Story line. Check each box as you complete the following steps.

THE UNIVERSAL STORY

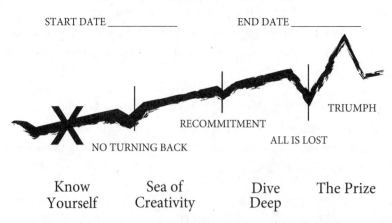

☐ Cross out the first quarter—Know Yourself. The work you did in phase 1 accomplished everything you needed for the beginning.

☐ Next, determine the date you plan to begin your first short-term creativity goal.

_____

☐ In phase 1, we talked about using one month as the deadline to reach your long-term goal. If that's the timeline you're comfortable with, count forward thirty days on your calendar from your start date to determine your end date. If you decide to try for a goal that won't take as long, use that target date instead. If you believe your efforts to achieve your goal warrant more time, choose a specific date to work toward. Again, constraint generates tension, which gives rise to ingenuity and accountability.

☐ What is the date you plan to complete your long-term creativity goal?

_____

THE UNIVERSAL STORY

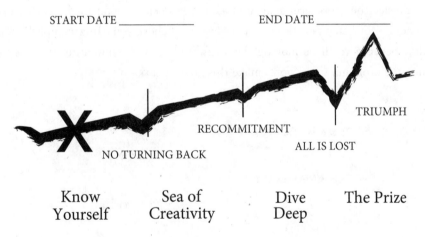

START DATE _____   END DATE _____

TRIUMPH

RECOMMITMENT

NO TURNING BACK   ALL IS LOST

Know   Sea of   Dive   The Prize
Yourself   Creativity   Deep

☐ Write the date you intend to begin above the first vertical line—No Turning Back.

☐ Write your proposed completion date above the highest peak of the Universal Story all the way to the right at nearly the very end.

THE UNIVERSAL STORY

CREATIVITY GOAL: MAKE A WOODCUT PRINT OF
ONE OF MY WATERCOLORS OR SKETCHES IN ONE MONTH

START DATE _____   END DATE _____

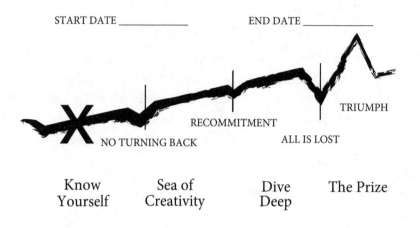

TRIUMPH

RECOMMITMENT

NO TURNING BACK   ALL IS LOST

Know   Sea of   Dive   The Prize
Yourself   Creativity   Deep

☐ Next, write your creativity goal as seen in the example above.

☐ Now, transfer the short-term goals and steps you decided upon in the earlier exercise onto sticky notes—one step per sticky note, unless you believe you can accomplish more than one per day. Because you'll be moving the steps, adding and eliminating steps as you progress through the program, sticky notes make this an easy task.

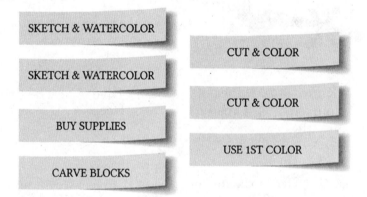

☐ Using a thirty-day plan, you have ten days total for each of the remaining three phases. Based on how many days per week you've decided to devote to your creativity, pace the sticky notes on the Universal Story accordingly. Consider the visual template that reflects your plan and adjust your short-term steps to align with what you realistically believe you're able to accomplish in the time frame. If needed, change your deadline to give yourself more time.

THE UNIVERSAL STORY

START DATE _____   END DATE _____

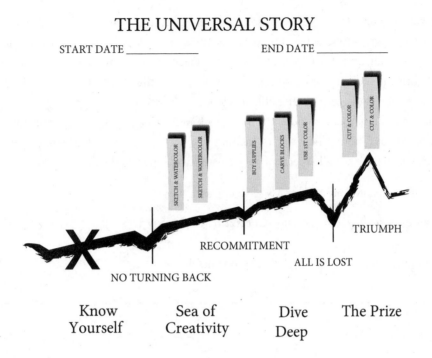

TRIUMPH

RECOMMITMENT

ALL IS LOST

NO TURNING BACK

Know
Yourself

Sea of
Creativity

Dive
Deep

The Prize

SPIRITUAL GOAL STRATEGIES

Using the Universal Story you created for your creativity goal, now map your spiritual goal. In the beginning, as you open yourself to new ideas, you're gripped with a plethora of emotions. List strategies below that you currently use to negotiate around self-sabotaging behaviors and beliefs. Along with things like meditation, walks in nature, playing with your children, washing the dog, yoga, massage, requesting help from a friend, and journaling, how do you unplug from the negative and connect to the good?

When in an undertow of confusing emotions, where do you turn for internal peace?

_____

_____

_____

_____

Did you include the spiritual pledge you created in step 4 as an avenue for internal peace?

Yes   *No*

You may have neglected to include your spiritual pledge. In time, you'll come to rely on your mantra. Rather than acting aggressively and feeding your weakness, your pledge helps you witness any self-sabotaging feelings, behavior, and attitudes you have as it washes over you, without shrinking away or lunging forward and fighting it and without belittling, discrediting, or getting caught up in it. With a keen awareness of your emotional state, you're better able to silence and disconnect from a part of your brain that's willing to harm and limit you. As you learn to control and direct your emotions to activate your best features, you teach your brain a new way of treating you with self-respect and self-love. As your inner dialogue shifts, you experience all aspects of your creativity willingly and without resistance.

"Insecurity doesn't control my actions. My self-confidence does."

"As a divine being worthy of success, my spirit is stronger than my fears."

If necessary, modify your inner spiritual pledge to yourself.

_____

_____

_____

_____

_____

Ignoring temptations and resisting distractions to show up for your creativity and engage with your spirit take practice and dedication. At the first sign of negativity, switch to chanting. Feeling scattered and unfocused? Chant. Set aside time daily to chant your mantra and connect to your higher self. Feel the joy and freedom that come when you're connected with your spirit and believing in yourself.

Below the Line

Everything that has to do with your inner spiritual goal belongs below the Universal Story line. Rather than use this space to anticipate steps and actions, this is where you

- indicate magic moments when you're in the creative flow,

- record what you did or thought (or didn't do or think) that you believe led to greater access to your imagination,

- assess your energy,

- assess your emotions,

- acknowledge moments when you trusted and followed your intuition, which led to greater productivity, and

- chart how often you use your spiritual pledge and why.

☐ Write a description of your best self. Say you're attempting to overcome your impatience and irritation while enacting the steps toward your long-term creativity goal. Write something about your new sense of patience, grace, and acceptance when faced with challenges and setbacks.

_____

_____

☐ Copy that description beneath the highest peak at the very end of the Universal Story.

THE UNIVERSAL STORY

START DATE _____   END DATE _____

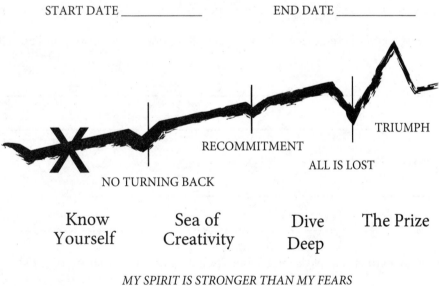

TRIUMPH

RECOMMITMENT

ALL IS LOST

NO TURNING BACK

Know Yourself   Sea of Creativity   Dive Deep   The Prize

MY SPIRIT IS STRONGER THAN MY FEARS
AND I DAILY SHOW UP FOR MY CREATIVITY WITH CONFIDENCE

☐ Write your spiritual pledge beneath the Universal Story line at the very beginning.

STAND BACK FROM YOUR UNIVERSAL STORY

Now, step back from your Universal Story. Without focusing on specific details, from a higher perspective and distant vantage point, take in your planned route or the big picture of what you plan for the next month—on both a practical and a spiritual level.

1. Compare action steps toward your creativity goal that threaten you to those you consider will be a breeze.

2. Consider the steps you believe most challenging as bumps in your journey and where you'll need to rely heavily on your spiritual pledge. Make notes beneath the Universal Story that line up with those bumps showing how best to ease your way forward.

3. Anticipate how the steps under your control support and strengthen your belief in yourself and your ability to take on the more difficult steps.

4. Assess how you paced your steps. Ensure you don't take on too much and burn out.

Appreciate that the Universal Story you designed brings you a multilayered attentiveness and allows for a unique perspective on developing the creative promise of your life.

Next, note your spiritual pledge below the line, and write down your observations on the page.

1. Compare what you've chosen to focus on with the description you wrote of your best self. I notice that:

_____

_____

2. Are the two connected?

_____

_____

3. What is the strength of your pledge in relationship to the creativity short-term goals?

_____

_____

4. Though your current pledge may not be enough to sustain you the entire journey, is what you plan to chant enough to get you started? Do you want to alter it at all?

_____

_____

TRANSFORMATION

You have plotted on the Universal Story the short-term goals, steps, and actions you plan to take toward your creativity goal, along with tracking your progress toward rewiring your brain and freeing your spirit. By doing this, you begin your creativity voyage with a transformational plan. This plan is designed to keep you organized and open your imagination and creativity, and to improve your productivity, which, in turn, transforms the quality of your work and your feelings about yourself. This plan is a declaration, and it gives you—and the forces within and outside you—a clear indication of what you're proposing to do and how.

With this clear idea of what you intend to do during each creative session you schedule for yourself, you don't need to spend precious time brainstorming what comes next. This early declaration allows you to begin each session open and free to accept and let come what wants to come.

Throughout the time you spend organizing the steps, continually speak your long-term goals out loud and in the present tense. Each time you chant your spiritual pledge, you reconnect to the spirited, natural part of you.

So…how do you feel about what you're about to take on? We discuss emotions in the next step of our program, but for now, write about your reaction to your plan and what you intend be doing for the next month.

_____

_____

_____

_____

_____

TAKE ACTION

1. Perform the first action step plotted above the line of your Universal Story toward your long-term creativity goal.

2. Under the Universal Story line that corresponds with the first action step, write how you're feeling. Repeat your spiritual pledge five times.

3. Begin tracking below the line of the Universal Story when you spot any flaws or negative behaviors in *you* and in *others*. Your goal here at the start is to become conscious of your mind habits throughout the day.

STEP 7

Your Emotional Set Point

Now that you've actually taken the first steps toward your external creativity goal, you're in the vortex of creativity. This is where emotions hang out—sharks, sting rays, and rip tides alongside mermaids, seahorses, and smooth sailing. Emotions define us, direct our actions, and express where we are in our spiritual evolution. Emotions have as much of a profound effect on what's being created and the artistic outcome as they have on the person creating the art. Emotions affect our energy and make us human.

The deeper you wade into your creativity, the more emotional you feel. Positive emotions fuel your energy and your desire to create. Negative emotions adversely affect your capacity to perceive and receive your intuitive vision. In criticism and fear, your powers of observation and ability to live in the creative moment are lost.

"I never appreciated how stubborn and closed-minded I could be, doing the same thing in the same way with no success. Now, I step away and use my creativity to come up with a solution."

"When I catch how critical and hard I am on myself and start to get depressed, I focus all my attention on my dedication and commitment to my goal."

What is your current relationship with emotions? Do you run from them by numbing yourself, or do you try to keep your emotions high through one artificial means or another—drugs, shopping, or keeping busy? Are you generally aware of how you're feeling?

_____

_____

_____

_____

Living a creative life forces you to examine and question and react differently to beliefs and conventions you've always held dear. Beliefs you once identified with and that gave you a sense of yourself are stripped away. This is not always easy. In fact, it can feel quite painful.

In order to truly understand how emotions affect creativity, it's time to explore all your emotions. Allow raw emotions out into the light. Become aware of the bodily sensations you experience around differing emotions. In learning how to access, accept, and embrace all your emotions, you're better able to use them in your art. Begin with your emotional state right now.

Write down the emotions you're feeling and the sensations in your body.

_____

_____

_____

_____

THREE PRIMARY EMOTIONS

Three emotions—fear, happiness, and sadness—create the physical sensations first to arrive in reaction to a situation. These three emotions are unthinking, instinctive responses we all share and are at the root of every other emotion. (I include anger as a secondary emotion and a direct outgrowth of fear.)

Which of the three primary emotions are you most familiar?

Happiness   *Sadness*   *Fear*

Out of these primary emotions sprout a multitude of other emotions called "secondary" and "tertiary emotions." When the primary emotions of fear or sorrow are expressed through a mixture of dark secondary and tertiary emotions, every imaginable drama results.

Dark Emotions

The following are descriptions of the first two types of primary emotions—fear and sorrow. Both fear and sadness are dark, because they represent lessons and challenges you are expected to meet, overcome, and learn from in preparation for the gift of your creativity goal. Fear and sadness often live in hard-to-reach, unexplored regions of your personality.

FEAR

Fear is a reaction to an imagined danger. Fear and all the secondary and tertiary emotions associated with it are dark or shadow emotions, because the meaning of their true nature is hidden and often buried.

"I'm afraid I won't stick with it long enough to reach the end."

"I worry no one will take my art and me seriously."

"I hate that [insert a secondary emotion of fear here] prevents me from moving forward."

Fear causes you to betray yourself and others; stay in emotionally damaging and power-draining relationships; look externally for money and security; bully, manipulate, and hurt others or yourself; hold onto experiences long after they're over; and dull the pain of living with the help of drugs, sex, and alcohol. Fear smothers creative will and aborts new ideas and passionate projects.

What is your earliest memory of feeling scared?

_____

_____

_____

_____

_____

_____

_____

Write about the last time you felt scared. Include what frightened you, the sensations you felt in your body, and what happened next.

_____

_____

_____

_____

_____

_____

List what frightens you in general, as well as fears directly related to your creativity.

_____

_____

_____

_____

_____

_____

_____

What was the scariest moment of your life?

_____

_____

_____

_____

_____

_____

_____

SADNESS

Sadness is the loss of control over a source of love or attention. Although sorrow is often considered a gateway to healing, it is generally classified as a shadow emotion. It activates sensations through your body to deaden the pain of not getting what you want or getting what you don't want.

"I get lonely creating all by myself and that makes me sad, and then I don't feel like finishing what I started."

"I feel sad that I don't always enjoy writing, drawing, dancing, or _____."

"I'm sad I'm not better at this."

You know you're feeling the primary emotion of sorrow when you have no energy, your voice is flat, you see nothing, your chin quivers, your chest hurts, the world around you turns dark, and you turn inward. Sadness, like fear, drains your spirit and your energy and often leads to physical complications. Fear worries something bad will come true. Sorrow believes it already has.

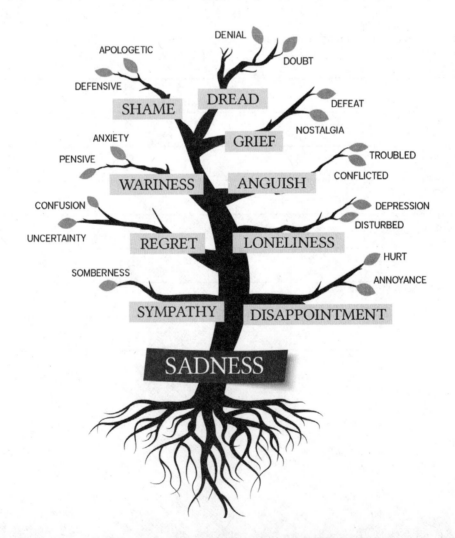

What is your earliest memory of feeling sad?

_____

_____

_____

_____

_____

_____

_____

Write about the last time you were sad. Include what made you sad, the sensations you felt in your body, and what happened next.

_____

_____

_____

_____

_____

_____

_____

List what makes you sad in general, as well as any sorrow that is directly related to your creativity.

_____

_____

_____

_____

_____

_____

_____

What was the saddest moment of your life?

_____

_____

_____

_____

_____

_____

Light Emotion

Unlike fear and sadness, which both represent repressed parts of your character, happiness is right out in the moment. However, similar to fear and sorrow, happiness shares the same propensity for being based on external circumstances. Happiness is a subjective state of mind; it can be gained and lost in a few moments, seconds, or hours. While sorrow and fear can become actual ways of life, happiness is susceptible to turning to dust in the face of anything that goes against our wants and desires.

HAPPINESS

We're happy when we achieve what we want. We're happy when we avoid what we don't want. Happiness is more vulnerable and fragile than the other two primary emotions.

"Time flies."

"The fun of creating and expressing myself restores me."

"I love the escape and discovering new things about myself."

Happiness is often overlaid with the secondary emotions of satisfaction and gratitude. Combined and mixed together, out of those light emotions come excitement, which has the potential to bloom into enthusiasm and elation. You know you're happy when you find yourself whistling for no apparent reason; you spontaneously and effortlessly complete something you've been putting off; and you feel positive, energized, and alert. You're grateful for little gestures and the sensory details in your everyday life.

What is your earliest memory of feeling happy?

_____

_____

_____

_____

_____

_____

_____

Write about the last time you were happy. Include what made you happy, the sensations you felt in your body, and what happened next.

_____

_____

_____

_____

_____

_____

_____

List what makes you happy in general as well as happiness that is directly related to your creativity.

_____

_____

_____

_____

_____

_____

_____

What is the happiest moment of your life so far?

_____

_____

_____

_____

_____

_____

_____

***

Now that we've covered the three primary emotions, let me ask you something. Imagine you saw someone crossing the street with a drooping posture, arms tucked in at his sides, a heavy step, downturned eyes, and wincing as a car approaches him at the crosswalk.

Which of the three primary emotions would you predict he's feeling?

Happiness   *Fear*   *Sadness*

In the same way, if people studied you crossing the street, which primary emotion might they say is yours?

Happiness   *Fear*   *Sadness*

The way you present yourself to the outside world reveals much about you emotionally.

EMOTIONAL SET POINT

Your emotional set point is the habitual emotion you seem to return to and where you typically reside. Your set point is your natural or conditioned internal system that fights to maintain a primary emotion in the face of changing external circumstances. Our emotional set point is like a touchstone by which we test the quality or genuineness of how we're feeling. Your emotional set point directly effects your creative expression.

Often, we're oblivious of the primary emotion in our race to react—lash out, cry, laugh, roar, sulk, or advise. Identifying your core emotion becomes even more challenging if you've never been taught about your emotions. Perhaps you were only allowed to feel happy—or at least show socially acceptable expressions of happiness—always smiling, complimenting others, saying please and thank you, reaching out to others, and acting faithfully courteous. Often, as children, any of the messy emotions—sadness, fear, anger, anxiety, and disappointment—are punished, bullied, or ignored.

Your emotional set point influences both the positive and negative habits you form. With a set point of fear, you develop habits to keep you safe—becoming overly cautious and suspicious when exposed to new ideas. Fear restricts you when you create. With a set point of sorrow, when faced with a creative challenge, you habitually turn passive and reserved. Sadness dulls your energy to create.

A grasp of your emotional set point helps explain what you project into your world both in your person and through your creativity. Sometimes it's easy to guess a creative's set point from their survey responses. Of course, only they know if I'm correct or if it was just how they were feeling that day. High-energy words like *excitement*, *hope*, and *love* point to happiness and, it's easy to imagine, creativity. Low-energy words like *shame*, *dread*, and *doubt* indicate a set point of sorrow and, it's easy to imagine, a resistance to create. Inflammatory energy such as *jealousy*, *hate*, and *blame* indicate a set point of fear and, it's easy to imagine, a rigidity to creativity. Whatever the set point, whether predetermined or preferred, the primary emotion we typically return to and that our personality and habits adjust to determines our subsequent emotional reactions.

When you think or speak about your creativity, what is the quality of your emotional state?

High energy   *Low energy*   *Inflammatory energy*

Your Personal Set Point

You take a bow to the applause and cheers. The love and approval cradles you with humility and gratitude. You feel safe and appreciate how wondrous life is until…your head hits the pillow that night. Then your thoughts turn dark as you return to your all-too-familiar emotional set point of fear and worry about a future when something bad will happen, is bound to happen, could happen, might happen. Or, before long, you return to sorrow. You feel sad, knowing you could have, should have done better. You compare your victory to those you've seen other creatives win, you believe that you've come up short, and your heart turns heavy.

What is the primary emotion that seldom seems to leave you?

Happiness   *Fear*   *Sadness*

The more familiar you become of your individual feelings, the less chance of your emotional set point becoming completely obscured by overlaying actions wrought of secondary and tertiary emotions. When you feel like you're losing control, do you relax, confident everything will work out in the end? Or do you do everything you can to avoid shame and regret mushrooming out of guilt? Perhaps you plant your feet far apart, jump to conclusions, and speak in anger. Then the question becomes: what are you afraid of?

Exploration

An exploration into the three primary emotions helps explain why you react as you do. Identification of your typical feelings and patterns leads to personal power. Slowly, you find yourself unplugging from the drama around you to search inside. You find you're able to control your emotions rather than be controlled by them. Beyond your emotions, the deeper, inner you—your spirit—waits…

Journal what a good day feels like while you're in the middle of productivity and steadily moving toward your goal.

_____

_____

_____

_____

_____

_____

_____

Journal what a low-energy, unproductive day feels like while you're in the middle of a downturn and overcome by dark emotions—blaming, shaming, depressed, resentful, fearful, and in doubt.

_____

_____

_____

_____

_____

_____

_____

Determine your set point by identifying which of the three primary emotions you always seem to return to—fear, sorrow, or happiness? If you're not sure which emotional set point best fits your emotional profile, periodically pause throughout your day and check how you're feeling. Don't look outside for answers. Look inward. As you do, run though the secondary and tertiary emotions on the three trees of primary emotions. Track your way to the root emotion.

Record your emotion first thing upon waking, every hour or so throughout the day, and then again before sleep.

_____

_____

_____

_____

_____

_____

_____

Based on what you find from the work you did above, now circle the primary emotion you believe represents your emotional set point:

Happiness   *Fear*   *Sadness*

Now that you're aware of your set point emotion, you may wish to revise your spiritual mantra.

_____

_____

_____

"*I refuse to allow fear run my life. I've got this!*"

"*When my energy turns dull, I stand up and dance and remind myself that I choose to be happy.*"

TAKE ACTION

- Continue performing action steps toward your creativity goal

- Continue tracking your use of your spiritual mantra below the Universal Story line that corresponds to the action step you're performing on the sticky note above the line.

- Continue filling in missing short-term steps for your creativity goal along the Universal Story line. The deeper you move toward your creativity goal, the more aware you become of the steps needed to reach it.

STEP 8

Subplots and Secondary Characters

The Sea of Creativity is also known as the sea of emotions. Like the Bermuda Triangle—a mythical part of the Atlantic Ocean where planes and ships mysteriously vanish—the Sea of Creativity has been blamed for the disappearance of thousands of creatives and their projects…never to be heard from again. This workbook is designed to address emotions and ensure that neither you nor your creative vision go missing.

Lurched and pitched about in the open sea, by now, you're likely windswept and even a bit seasick. You're quickly finding that making the necessary adjustments in your life to accommodate your pursuit of your goal isn't that easy. Turn your focus to people you interact with, as well as to the responsibilities you shoulder, that have the potential to either encourage your creativity or kill it.

In stories, a subplot is a side story that supports and enhances the main story. At this point in our program, your pursuit of your creativity goal may be a subplot you're hoping will enhance your main life as a student, wife, researcher, father, engineer, doctor, daughter, teacher, first-responder, or astronaut. As you become more deeply involved with your goal, your creativity may, in fact, become the main story of your life.

Currently, what is the main story of your life?

_____

_____

_____

Subplots in our lives connect to our main story and are linked together through a particular meaning. With you as the main character of your life, secondary characters—both those who support you and those who oppose you—populate your subplots. Every person who makes up a subplot in your life and your main story has significance to your spiritual journey. They reflect and bring a deeper understanding of where you currently stand in your overall spiritual development.

As you adapt to living creatively and how you typically spend your days, the people in your life are expected to adjust their expectations of you and adapt as well. These adjustments and adaptations are apt to elicit dark emotions in you and also in those around you.

IDENTIFY YOUR MAJOR SUBPLOTS

Many of us glide along the surface of socially acceptable parameters as decided by our role in our family, career, and community and among those who surround us. Doing things as they've always been done—writing stories that mirror the stories you read and love, snapping photos of views you've seen before, painting pictures of conventional images—is typical. More difficult is to move beyond socially and culturally acceptable creativity to your absolute truth.

Creativity asks that rather than follow others, you instead become a trailblazer into new realms. To access the innermost creativity that is yours and yours alone, first it's helpful to determine the major subplots and characters in your life and their influence over you. Let's try that now.

1. Place yourself at the level of the main plot of your life and list all the different subplots and commitments and habits that currently come before your creative life—your marriage, family, job, volunteer work, the classes you take, the internet and social media, exercise, shopping, caring for others, and so forth.

_____

_____

_____

_____

_____

2. Next to each of the subplots you listed above, include how much time daily or weekly you devote to each of them.

Sacrifice

Is the need to eliminate something to make time for your creativity goal, at least during this goal cycle, immediately obvious?

Yes   *No*

Sacrificing something you like makes room for something you love—your creativity. The notion of giving up something old to make room for something new in your life is an ancient purging ritual.

One creative, when looking over her list of subplots, noticed how much time she spent volunteering. Though she likes helping others with no thought of financial reward, she also realized that she was devoting her energy to causes as a way to fill up her days in what are considered conventionally acceptable ways. As she began to shift her priorities and open up time for her creativity, she felt her spirit blossom in ways new to her.

Another creative I worked with suddenly understood how much time he spent playing games on his phone. As a ritual to show his commitment to himself and his creativity, he canceled and opted out of all the gaming apps he'd accumulated.

Take a moment to consider your subplots and the commitments you listed above. Is there a subplot (or more than one) you can easily and painlessly give up or cut back on to free more time for your creativity today?

Yes   **No**

If yes, list them.

_____

_____

_____

_____

Many of us have been taught to put others ahead of us and do for others first. All of those people and projects you place ahead of yourself become main plots in your life with *you* relegated to subplot status. Traditionally, people who put personal needs first are viewed as selfish and self-centered.

This negative perception changed for me on a flight from San Francisco to Phoenix for a speaking engagement. I was sitting in an aisle seat next to a mother and her child. If not for the mother and child next to me, I may have again missed the significance of the airline attendant's directive to place the mask over your own face before attending to your child. Makes perfect sense: if you die helping your child, you won't be there when the child needs you the most.

"Up until now, I've always put my writing second to family, friends, and outside work. Now, I try to put it first unless there is an absolute need to do otherwise. I consider writing time as my gift to myself."

"I've learned that I easily commit to others while I have trouble committing to myself! I now block out time on my calendar to devote to my creative exploration. That way, if I choose to do something else, I'm making that choice consciously."

Precious Energy

You're no good to anyone when you give up your hopes and dreams and creativity to devote all your precious energy to others. If this is true for you, then, whether resentment, unhappiness, apathy, blame, regret, and even anger are actually expressed or consciously experienced, you weave your energy into every action you take and risk perpetuating unhappiness for generations to come.

The quality of your spiritual energy as you travel the Universal Story is decided by your thoughts and emotions, beliefs and patterns. In other words…you. Spiritual energy is viewed two ways.

Dark energy. Dark energy symbolizes a gloomy and shadowy time to be alone and withdrawn. Any negative and frazzled feelings you drag around with you also drags down your creativity and your energy to create.

Light energy. Light energy reflects joy and ease and a weightless, nimble brightness. Centered, balanced, and fulfilled, you send out positive energy into the world.

In this workbook, you're asked to put yourself first. Prove you're committed to your creativity by making sacrifices to get what you want. Eliminating something habitual and numbing is no picnic. The more ego satisfaction you garner from financial gain, community approval, and the love of others, the more difficult—and worthwhile—the sacrifice.

Consider again your subplots and the commitments you listed above. Star the subplots you're willing to eliminate or negotiate for more time. Write down an action plan to free up more time for your creativity.

Social Media

With social media and smart phones, most of us are hard-pressed to go an entire day without checking in to some form of communication. For many people, interacting through technology has become obsessive. The problem for creatives is that interruptions from your phone yank you from the semi-meditative zone you relax into when creating. If you're invested in keeping up on social media, and you find, when checking in, that you've lost followers, a rush of panic fills you. Disoriented, and having lost the momentum into the deep work of your creative task, you decide to put off your short-term creative step for later—perhaps even wait until tomorrow.

Daily, for one week, track how often you're on your devices other than using them for creative purposes.

Monday _____

Tuesday _____

Wednesday _____

Thursday _____

Friday _____

Saturday _____

Sunday _____

If you're not ready to break your addiction to your electronic devices or simply turn them off during your creativity sessions, perhaps in time you will be. For the rest of you, I'm hoping what to give up is suddenly quite obvious and, in the same instant, a relief.

Decide when and for how long you'll devote to your devices. Write your answers as a commitment statement.

_____

_____

_____

_____

_____

Or consider fulfilling one action step on your Universal Story first and then reward yourself by answering emails and responding to social media.

Just One More Thing

I don't want your creativity and spiritual goals to be yet another subplot and something else to cram into your day, to worry about, and to beat yourself up over, if you don't accomplish what you set out to do one day (or many). Decide every day whether to create or not. Whichever way you decide, you have the power to live as you choose. Enjoy yourself.

Creativity and spiritual goals are meant to enhance your life, not detract from it; feed your energy, not add to your fatigue; and liberate your unconscious potential, not undermine it. Your creativity and spiritual goals are intended to bring a radiance and wholeness to every aspect of your life.

Go back over your list of subplots and see if you can pare back even more. This time, list only your essential subplots and leave all else off your list.

_____

_____

_____

_____

_____

_____

Give yourself the time you need as you dismantle your priorities and begin shifting the way you look at your days, what you commit to, and how you schedule yourself. Create an environment that best nurtures your creativity and enthusiasm for creating. Wedge your steps into every spare moment. You achieve your goals not by giving up the challenge, but by giving up the comfort.

Don't be surprised, as you begin to move from your head to your heart and into your best creative life, that you often find your hands sweaty, your heart palpitating, and your knees quivering. To break the spell that your career, family, relationships, and prevailing cultural norms have you under requires boldness and courage. Each step forward empowers and expands you with the belief you can do anything—most of all, manifest your dreams and desires.

IDENTIFY SECONDARY CHARACTERS IN YOUR LIFE

People who are secondary to you reflect lessons you're here to learn. Many people believe that we choose our families. That everyone in your life is actually a mirror reflecting beliefs and behaviors and attitudes that you embody. Often we believe we're seeing other people's bad habits or limited ideas without knowing that we, too, reflect those same patterns and beliefs.

List all the major and secondary people you interact with on a regular basis.

_____

_____

_____

_____

_____

_____

_____

_____

_____

_____

A Different Way to View People in Your Life

You meet, interact with, and work with lots of people in a day. Most of those people have little or no effect—positive or negative—on you. However, others elicit strong feelings—positive and negative. Let us, for a moment, embrace the idea that these people have been sent into your life not randomly, but with a spiritual purpose. These relationships are best viewed symbolically.

Positive Effect. Every person you admire and who delights, inspires, and motivates you embodies qualities and possibilities that are sleeping or unrealized in you. These people are nonthreatening. You feel safe with them. Their support, friendliness, and helpfulness bring out the best in you and afford you the space to demonstrate your higher self. You're able to respond to them in healthy and functional ways.

List the friends and family and coworkers with whom you most easily share your love, strength, and positive energy. Include the traits they embody that you most admire. Make a check mark above the traits you believe you share or have in common with them.

_____

_____

_____

_____

_____

_____

Negative Effect. Now, turn to people who bring out the worst in you. The quality of the energy you exchange with them is negative and often, after encounters with them, you beat yourself up for flying off the handle, lashing out, or acting rude or snobbish, and you wish you could take back your words. Or they simply leave you tired and uninspired. All of these reactions indicate that when interacting, you lose your own personal power. Your spiritual journey involves taking back your energy and power.

Make a list of anyone who always seems to elicit negative feelings in you. Include those feelings next to that person.

_____

_____

_____

_____

_____

_____

_____

Just as with all opposition where we lose our individual power, these people force us to learn about ourselves in ways no one else can. Far more than the positive relationships you have, these conflicted relationships offer opportunities for us to change. You decide whether that change is negative—in that they cause you to shut down or become bitter and negative—or you decide to learn and grow and heal by seeing in them what you don't like about yourself and by then acting differently.

Refer back to your list of difficult people who bring up negative energy in you. Now, write what about them tries your patience or irritates you, frustrates or angers you. Explore the characteristics, mannerisms, or behaviors you have in common with them. Or perhaps they remind you of something you did in the past that you feel guilty about, something you'd rather forget. Journal what you discover.

_____

_____

_____

_____

_____

Whether friends or foes to your creativity, secondary characters benefit you when you establish clear boundaries around your creative time. The challenge for you then becomes respecting your own boundaries. If your family and friends see you squander your time, they begin testing to see how far they can push your limits. Through commitment, you protect your schedule.

SYNCHRONICITY

You peel off sticky notes from above the Universal Story line and enact your short-term action goals. You're energized and feeling that you are playing the part of the conscious artist—doing what you set out to do. Suddenly, everything you read in the news has relevance to your goal. Conversations you hear and shapes and textures you see inform your art. Everywhere you turn, you're encouraged with gifts. Synchronicity lures you forward. Knowing how fragile beginnings are, forces within and without support you. Before long, they won't be quite as cooperative. For now, you're enthusiastic and living the dream.

As you perform the steps for each task you set out for yourself, how do you feel?

   Antsy   *Analytical*   *Critical*   *Buoyant*   *Exuberant*   *Lost in the moment*

TAKE ACTION

Every day, continue to track your use of your spiritual mantra below the Universal Story line that corresponds to the action step you're performing that is above the line. Move sticky notes with action steps you miss further along on the line. Reassess what you're doing to determine which of your actions are working toward success. Adapt your inner spiritual goal or add to the one you've already created to better support your progress.

Every night before going to sleep, visualize the next day and the activities you have planned and outlined on your Universal Story line to achieve your goals. See yourself doing what you set out to do. Feel the wood-carving knife or paintbrush in your hand. Smell the wood chips or paint thinner. See the wood grain or colors you apply.

Track the nights you visualize the next day well and how the results match up the next day.

_____

_____

_____

_____

_____

_____

_____

_____

_____

_____

_____

STEP 9

Self-Awareness, Lessons, Skills, Knowledge, and Experience

By now in our program toward boundless creativity, you're deep into your creative life. Based on our thirty-day deadline, if you scheduled every day for your creativity and each day accomplished one new step, you've accomplished six or so of the steps you plotted along this phase on your Universal Story.

You've tracked how you've faithfully chanted your spiritual pledge countless times throughout the day and night. You're beginning to draw power and confidence from your strengths. Your face is flushed, knowing that anything is possible. You find yourself grinning and humming a happy tune.

Jot down your successes so far with your creativity steps. Include how you feel about your progress.

_____

_____

_____

_____

_____

Have you learned anything about yourself and your spirit from chanting your pledge?

Yes   *No*

If yes, explain. (If you have yet to learn anything new about yourself, continue chanting. In time you will.)

_____

_____

_____

SETBACKS AND LESSONS

If you haven't already, eventually, quickly or slowly, you become aware of what you don't know—about your chosen form of creative expression, yourself, or both. These needs come out of necessity or are forced upon you through setbacks.

This early middle phase of our program signals a time of learning lessons and new skills; gaining experience and knowledge about your craft, creativity, and those around you; increasing your self-awareness; and managing your emotions as you pursue your external goal.

For now, simply list any areas in your chosen medium where you're feeling you may need a better understand of the art, a deeper insight into what you're attempting to achieve, or new skills to develop. Or perhaps you're becoming painfully aware of parts of your belief system about your inner worth that need to be uncovered in order to progress.

What do you need to learn or uncover?

_____

_____

_____

_____

_____

Rest assured that stumbling blocks are part of the creative process and to be expected. Their main objective is to pause your forward progress, not to send you into a tailspin, but rather to alert you of something you're missing for success. As difficult as they may seem at the time, setbacks always come with gifts of wisdom, knowledge, experience, and learning.

Imagine your dream is to be a wood carver. You've spent days carving, and as a stooped old man slowly appears, you're jubilant. And then your knife slips. Do you throw the piece of wood across the room—certain that the piece is ruined—and stomp away angry about your clumsiness (demonstrating fear you *will never be* good enough for the medium you love)? Or say you mix a color on your palette that creates a mystical lighting on your painting. Exhausted, you leave the piece to finish the next day. In the morning, upon finding the mix of colors hardened and unusable, you begin to cry (demonstrating sorrow that you *aren't* good enough for the medium you love)? In each case, the creative has experienced a setback.

What lessons about your creativity are you learning?

_____

_____

_____

_____

_____

Spinning Ahead

A common setback involves spinning ahead of yourself with worry about what will be required of you down the line. One creative stopped writing what she envisioned was the first book in a trilogy because she suddenly became fixated on the belief that she wouldn't be able to imagine enough scenes for the next two books. Another creative sabotaged herself as she started obsessing about how she'd manage when lots of people wanted to buy her art.

> *"How will I manage all the bookkeeping and still do what I love? What if so many people order prints that I'm not able to fulfill the orders fast enough?"*

In both cases, these creatives jumped too far ahead and placed their concerns about the future ahead of their present-day abilities. These are valuable lessons learned along the way toward your creativity goal—lessons all creatives are confronted with and are required to master.

1. List any setbacks you're experiencing.

_____

_____

_____

_____

_____

2. For each one, indicate the severity of the setback with a rating of "minor," "manageable," or "major."

3. Next to each setback, add the emotions it causes in you.

4. Locate each emotion on the emotion trees in step 7 and write the primary emotion next to each setback.

5. Now, explore what each setback is attempting to communicate to you about what you're missing and need to learn, develop, and experience. (Refer to the list you generated in the previous section.) Brainstorm solutions. List those solutions.

_____

_____

_____

_____

_____

_____

6. Next to each solution, add the emotions they elicit in you.

7. Locate each emotion on the emotion trees in step 7 and write the primary emotion next to each solution.

8. Do you notice any difference between the emotions the setbacks create versus how the solutions make you feel? Journal about your findings.

_____

_____

_____

_____

_____

_____

SKILLS AND KNOWLEDGE

Creatives continually encounter unanticipated elements of creativity—this is where growth and transformation take place.

Add to your Universal Story the solution steps you brainstorm to take toward your long-term creativity goal. Include steps to research and find the necessary help you need.

If you have enough time in your schedule, fulfill these additional steps while also faithfully following your original short-term steps. If you're unable to do both the new steps while staying true to your schedule and make your deadline, give yourself more time by changing your deadline or cutting back on your expectations.

What's important is not when you finish but what you're learning. Rather than tensing up, allow yourself the freedom to make mistakes, and slow down after each misstep to glean the lesson presented about your craft and about yourself.

SELF-AWARENESS

By far, the greatest setbacks you're likely to experience are internal. The longer you stick with your creative goals, the more challenged you find yourself. Becoming conscious of how and when you sabotage yourself isn't always easy. The key is not to become discouraged but to be invigorated and strengthened by the challenges. Yet, sadly, for many creatives, this is not the case.

How do you stand in the way of your creativity?

_____

_____

_____

_____

To move beyond the way you censor your artistic expression and instead to live in belief and to own your power, first you have to actually be conscious of how you sabotage yourself. Most disruptive feelings and emotions and habits are so ingrained that we don't know they're there, working against us.

These embedded and well-established mind habits need to be rooted out and transformed or dramatically altered before you can truly succeed at your goal. Without changing these habits, any success or achievement you have will be short-lived, because you will begin to tear yourself down and find reasons why your accomplishments aren't good enough. If you believe you don't deserve your achievements, you'll find ways to diminish your triumphs.

What is the prevalent mind habit that works against you?

_____

_____

_____

_____

CELEBRATE

For now and throughout the middle of the Universal Story, when you spot unproductive mind habits and find you're out of sync with the person you are striving to be, celebrate! This is a huge step. You're becoming conscious of your inner self. Rather than fall into the trap of blaming and criticizing yourself, acting harshly and complaining about yourself, you deserve to congratulate yourself. Trust that change is occurring.

> *"I've learned to put my inner critic that tells me I'm not good enough in the time-out corner and ignore it for the most part."*

It's not easy to slow the momentum of your mind habits and emotional reactions long enough first to become conscious of them and next to turn them in the direction you wish them to go. Yet just as they were created, your thoughts and beliefs and emotions can also be dismantled. The first step—learning to stop, wait, and listen to the inner voice of your ancient and timeless spirit—is transformational. In time, you learn to make friends with your emotions and habits. Ultimately, you experiment with thinking and acting in new ways.

Describe how you act when facing an obstacle.

_____

_____

_____

_____

What do you tell yourself when hit with a setback?

_____

_____

_____

_____

_____

If you answered with your spiritual mantra, congratulations! If you answered that you try to understand what you're feeling and saying internally, well done! Truly. These are signs that you're willing to pay attention without judgment but rather with full acceptance.

If you haven't yet reached that point, give yourself time and recommit to the process. Breathe into the feelings and messages. And then…most importantly, transform your embedded belief system into strength and beauty with the help of your spiritual pledge.

Negative habits and beliefs develop over time. The longer you practice them, the more calcified they become. Attempting to release what holds you back may incite an internal war between your current wish to change and the deep-seeded need to refuse your true destiny. The only way to resolve the battle is to start loving and approving of yourself, which ultimately floods into the loving and approving of all others.

Quick—write your initial response to what you just read about loving and approving of yourself.

_____

_____

_____

_____

_____

How easy is it to love and approve of yourself?

Impossible   *Hard*   *Complicated*   *Feasible*   *Easy*

It takes patience to work through and replace all that holds you back.

Reciting Your Spiritual Mantra

To help with this loving approach, think of your inner spiritual goal as an oath or solemn promise to yourself. In repeating your spiritual pledge, you call upon your spirit to witness your truth in sincerely intending to do what you say. Your oath helps penetrate your fog of self-doubt so you can focus on believing in yourself. It allows you to immediately reorient yourself.

Right now, without looking, chant your spirit pledge. Do you remember it?   *Yes*   *No*

Do the words roll off your tongue?   *Yes*   *No*

Rewrite your spiritual pledge.

_____

_____

_____

Your spiritual oath is as an explicit statement with the power to change your life. It's a reminder that you want this. Each time you make the pledge to yourself, you foster the ability to step back, take a breath, and examine options for the best way forward.

"I override my urge to procrastinate by marveling at my ability to fill up a blank page with valuable information."

"I move out of fear and into enthusiasm and joy."

ALIGN WITH YOUR SPIRIT

The more aligned you are with your spirit, the easier it is to understand what it is saying. Enhance the pathway to your spirit with the use of your spirit mantra. We're attempting alchemy by burning away all the baggage you've accumulated over the years that holds you back; doing this will bring forth your best self—the gold.

Before you recommit to your creative goal at the end of the next step, again evaluate your spiritual oath. You may find your affirmation isn't powerful enough to lift you over the hurdles you're encountering.

If you've found a way to strengthen what to say to accept your shortcomings and support your strengths, adjust your spiritual affirmation. Write it here.

_____

_____

Tape your spiritual pledge to your refrigerator, your computer monitor, and the dashboard of your car. Carry it with you always if only as a constant reminder. Throughout the day, reprogram your inner dialogue by repeatedly chanting your oath: while you drive, as you exercise, and when you're simply hanging out. Keep directing your attention and energy into your new belief system.

Take time now to write your revised spiritual affirmation below the line on your Universal Story where you're currently working. If necessary, also change the statement of your best self at the end of the voyage. By tracking your use of your spiritual mantra, in the end, you have a timeline of your spiritual progress.

Keep the Faith

Continue returning to your spiritual pledge. By exercising authority over your emotional traps with your confident and forceful explicit statement of belief in yourself, more and more you understand how self-doubt and emotional traps make you lose touch with the reality and bigger picture of who you really are. Slowly, your spiritual proclamation becomes a self-realized inner truth.

Is this indeed happening for you? Write down how it's happening. Do you find your self-doubt lifting? Are you choosing to banish emotional traps from your life? Are you keeping the reality of your strengths front and center? Is your spiritual pledge making you stronger?

_____

_____

_____

_____

_____

_____

Consider your spiritual pledge as a pep talk. By replacing counter-productive habits with positive ones, you rewire your brain. Think the chanting won't work, isn't working, isn't enough to help? Try it anyway.

As you create and become aware of your feelings, habits, and beliefs, journal what you find. Moments while you're innovating are opportunities to wake up to your inner self. Don't judge what you discover. Jot it down.

_____

_____

_____

_____

_____

How many times do you currently repeat your spiritual mantra during the day?

| 1 | 5 | 10 | 20 | 200 | *more* |

RESISTANCE

One morning, with a crystal blue sky stretching in all directions, I strolled along the bluff overlooking Monterey Bay, where I live. A car pulled up beside to me, and the driver buzzed down his window and asked for directions. As I started to give them, he immediately interrupted me with his version. I tried to point out where he was wrong, but, though he was asking for help, he was so sure of himself that he interrupted and repeated his version. It took me a several attempts before I understood that he couldn't hear me until he admitted to himself that he was confused.

Are you open to help and guidance?   *Yes*   *No*

The more rigidly you believe that the way you've always done things is the only way, the more you'll miss meaningful guidance and help. You can't change a bad habit—giving up and giving in, or belittling and discrediting what you're creating—until you're able to acknowledge when you're doing it. You can't erase the destructive mind habit of fear and self-doubt until you're aware of when you feel that way. In order to live your best creative life, denial is no longer an option. As empowering as your forward progress toward your external goal is, even more valuable is discovering your habitual state of mind. With a belief that you can overcome your internal negativity, you will.

Track when and what you're doing when you spot your flaws or negative behaviors.

_____

_____

_____

_____

At the same time, track when and what you're doing when you spot your strengths.

_____

_____

_____

_____

DAYDREAMING

Another common setback creatives experience during this part of the voyage is simply being unable to imagine the next step, the next scene, or the next stroke. You're left feeling that your creativity has dried up. There are several ways to combat this. One is to seek an answer from your dreaming mind—either when you are asleep or awake.

The veil between awake and asleep is a major portal with the potential to bring the answers and support you need. Ask for help or an answer just as you're about to go all the way under into sleep. Ask to be shown in ways that demonstrate you've been heard.

You can also seed your daydreaming. Give yourself the gift of quiet introspection. Daydreams take you on a journey into the future. Try it now.

Sit overlooking the sea or next to a shady river or simply where you currently are. Plant your feet on the ground. Let your hands lie loosely in your lap. Take a few deep, cleansing breaths. Close your eyes and relax with no expectation. Let go of all other thoughts as you ask for help. Then quietly wait. Listen.

After you open your eyes, but before you're completely alert, take a moment to write what you learned.

_____

_____

_____

_____

Close your eyes again and take a moment to watch yourself in your imagination, as if you're watching a movie. What's different about you since you started this program? What's the same? What needs to change to get you where you wish to be?

_____

_____

_____

_____

List how you most enjoy nourishing your creative spirit and allowing yourself room for introspection, such as digging in the dirt, listening to uplifting music, wandering through art galleries and museums, or creating rituals.

_____

_____

_____

_____

Keep Your Vision to Yourself

Ultimately, you'll be asked to share what you create with others. Here, in the early part of creating your vision, keep your creative dream to yourself. Your true vision is too new and fragile and unformed to subject it to others' opinions. Let creativity become your truth. Use art to tell the story of your spirit. Healing comes in bits and pieces. You're attempting to birth a creative life that honors all parts of you.

Remember who you are. Be loyal to yourself. Honor your creativity, and you will have all the support you need to go the distance.

Now that you've had a chance to work on the beginning steps you mapped out on your Universal Story line, take time to evaluate the habits you're finding that *prevent* you from showing up consistently for your creativity.

_____

_____

_____

_____

_____

Now that you've had a chance to work on the beginning steps you mapped out on your Universal Story, take time to evaluate the habits you're finding that *support* you in showing up consistently for your creativity.

_____

_____

_____

_____

_____

Are you having fun yet?   *Yes*   *No*

TAKE ACTION

Stand back from your Universal Story and assess how you've paced your short-term steps. Mark places on your Universal Story where you can disembark for a bit of daydreaming. As you do, continue to fill in missing short-term steps for your creativity goal. The deeper you move toward your creativity goal, the more aware you become of the steps needed to reach it.

STEP 10

The Need to Recommit to Your Creative Goals

THE UNIVERSAL STORY

RECOMMITMENT

Sea of   Dive
Creativity   Deep

You've arrived at the second major energy marker in the Universal Story—Recommitment, also know as Renewal. From the challenges you've faced developing a relationship with your art, you may well understand the need to recommit to your goals. First, let's take a moment to summarize the ideal model of what you've accomplished thus far in the program.

If you've given yourself a one-month deadline, you've completed ten steps, more or less, toward your creativity goal. You've found solace though the use of your spiritual oath, having time and time again invoked it as a divine witness of the truth of your determination. Each time you come face-to-face with a flaw or weakness in yourself, you pause, remind yourself of your strengths, and confirm your relationship with the most vital part of yourself—your spirit. As you ride the wave of creative momentum, everything else disappears, and nothing else matters.

Does that describe you?   *Yes*   *No*

If yes, pat yourself on the back for a job well done. Dance and celebrate that you're staying true to your commitment and living a creative life. Keep going and don't look back! If you answered no, read on (and even if you answered yes, read on—as you'll find yourself struggling eventually).

NOT HAPPENING FOR YOU

Much more common than the above depiction is finding that the excitement you felt starting this program has turned into a dizzying dance of ebb and flow. One day, the reality of what you've undertaken drags on your initial enthusiasm. The next day, you're back in the flow of creativity. Then, suddenly, the thrill disappears again. You have no idea where it went or how to get it back. A few days later, without warning, the creative whisper awakens you, nagging at your heart to hurry home to your creativity. But before you know it, a sense of boredom and lethargy sets in.

Are you experiencing similar ups and downs of emotions?   *Yes*   *No*

For most of us, doubt steals in as the excitement of beginning wanes. You're dismayed to find how weak your execution is compared to your vision. Rather than hole up alone with your creativity, you give in when friends pressure you to go to lunch. You've fallen behind on your steps and feel like a failure. You waver when you hear how you're the only one who can chair the committee you served on last year. You're dismayed when you realize how far you are from completion. You feel guilty when your kids ask why isn't dinner ready yet? You question yourself when a sibling asks, "Who do you think you are—Georgia O'Keeffe?"

You've repeated your spiritual statement a thousand times. Sometimes it encourages and uplifts you. Other times, the practice feels silly and inconsequential. One day, your self-sabotaging and negative thoughts lessen. The next, the belittling, critical, and bullying voice in your head seems to surge unchecked.

You long to find wholeness and completion though acceptance of all parts of yourself, but rather than a form of loving healing, you wonder why you even started this program. You find yourself moaning about how impossible your goal is, how no one will notice, no one is going to care about what you create. But the truth is that until you complete what you set out to accomplish, you do not know what's going to happen at the end.

Are you beginning to doubt yourself or are you confident about going forward?

Doubting   *Confident*

Seasick from the rocking and sloshing emotions, more and more you look back longingly at your old familiar territory. The pushback you receive from people around you and from yourself startles you. You're tempted to give up, retreat, or delay your creativity goal. Before you do, remember the Sea of Creativity is also known as the sea of emotion.

What you're experiencing is a vital part of the creative process. Instead of being controlled by your emotions, learning what sets you off gives you the opportunity to lift yourself up and change rather than stomp yourself down. For the next several days, do the following exercise.

1. Take a moment to journal about the emotions you feel when in the flow. Keep track of what you're doing when you're up.

    _____

    _____

    _____

    _____

    _____

    _____

2. Now, follow the emotions on the emotion trees in step 7 to the root or primary emotion. Note the pattern in your emotional responses when you're freely creating.

3. Next, note how you feel when disenchanted with your creativity goal. Keep track of what you're doing when you're down.

    _____

    _____

    _____

    _____

    _____

    _____

4. Follow the emotions on the emotion trees in step 7 to the root or primary emotion. Note the pattern in your emotional responses when the step you're on creates stress in you.

5. See if you can find a pattern in the steps that make you feel good and successful as opposed to the steps that make you feel drained and like a failure.

_____

_____

_____

_____

Have you ever noticed that the core in the word emotion is motion? No wonder you're rocking and rolling.

Rank your use of your mantra (10 = you repeat it all the time and 1 = you seldom or never repeat it).

1   2   3   4   5   6   7   8   9   10

THE EBB AND FLOW IN EVERY CREATIVE SPIRITUAL VOYAGE

No matter how fabulous and productive and successful, the outgoing energy eventually must return. The creative flow sends you flying forward, but you also need empty space. In the luxury of silence, we release what was, imagine what can be, and rest. Ultimately, the ebb, as much as the flow, is a vital part of living a creative life.

In our relentless surge forward, we often miss what is covered over and hidden from us. Rather than experience ebbs as setbacks, see them as opportunities to relax and thus create openings for your spirit to communicate with you. Just because you're having a rough day, it doesn't mean you're not meant for success. So you're lost and don't know what to do next. This is no time to give up. Just as each part of the cycle of the tides is valid, each part of a creative life is valid. The energy recedes and returns eternally.

Acknowledge when you're in the ebb of your creativity. Accept this part of the cycle and recommit to yourself. Don't run from it or change it. Don't start planning for a future of scarcity and loss. Rather, accept setbacks, confusion, loss, aloneness, and moments when your energy ebbs as times of inner stillness. In acceptance, you're able to use the time to rest and explore what is hiding in the dark. Bringing what holds you back out into the light replenishes and prepares you for the coming flow. You're better able to live in balance trusting that the energy will again flow.

So long as you continue to rely on your habit of showing up and working on your pottery, the musical instrument you're learning to play, or your involvement in community theater, you're living a creative life.

Without worrying about the waxing and waning of the creative life, so long as you believe in yourself and continue to recommit, results will come to you.

When did you last allow yourself to freely enjoy some alone time with absolutely no pressure? Write down what you did during that time: daydream, wander, splash in the puddles, or sing and dance all alone? Journal what you learned about yourself during that time on your own and if the free time fostered your ability to stick with your creativity goal.

_____

_____

_____

_____

_____

Jot down what tempts you to retreat, give up, or delay your goal.

_____

_____

_____

_____

Are you succeeding in your efforts to limit the activities and commitments and obligations of daily life to make room for your creativity? Write about how you're doing with putting yourself and your creativity first.

_____

_____

_____

_____

_____

Fear that an Ebb Signifies Failure

When stuck in our creative life, we're afraid the flow is never coming back. An emotional ebb feels like abandonment and a sign that we're not meant for success. Diminished, we forget the mantra wise women and men have chanted throughout history—*this too will pass*. There will be times of ebb. The flow always returns.

Living at the beach, I witness daily just how dramatic the ebb and flow of the tide is. Surging king tides cover everything in their path. Drama roars on the surface with whitecaps and crashing waves. A receding tide returns a sense of calm and reveals the shore and all sorts of treasures left behind for the finding.

When in the creative flow, we move quickly and effortlessly. We're energized, pumped, passionate, and enthusiastic. We act and react. Then, without warning, we falter, stub our toe, lose our momentum, get sick, feel weak, and begin to doubt.

The truth is that you're repeatedly being tested and asked to recommit to your creative goals, which, in reality, is recommitting to *yourself* over and over again. If your goals are easy to achieve, you don't stretch and grow and find out just how strong and powerful you really are. The problem is that the more personal responsibility you take for how you act and who you are—warts and all—the messier and more upsetting your life. As one creative said, "I'm sick of taking responsibility for everything that happens to me. I just want the pain to go away. There must be a pill for it. Working on myself is tiresome. I don't feel like I'm getting anywhere."

The only way to change is not by taking a pill or running back to the old way but by accepting all parts of you and keeping going. What we are striving toward is not accomplished in one step or even one hundred steps. Yet every step, whether forward or backward, uncovers more and more of your inner world. As with changing any habit, time is needed to

- become aware,

- explore, and

- replace the old with the new, over and over again.

Suddenly you begin to notice new beliefs and behaviors integrating and becoming second nature to you. Warmth rushes through your body.

For now, close each creativity session while you're still in the flow—after you've made a successful cut in a carving or written a lovely section in a musical score. Stop what you're doing while feeling good about yourself and the process of creating something out of nothing. Close each session before you lose energy or have a chance to trash-talk your work. Instead, stop while you're still excited about what comes next but before actually launching into the steps.

Track how the above suggestions work for you as you finish each creative session over the next several days.

_____

_____

_____

_____

_____

_____

THRESHOLD GUARDIANS

Gatekeepers guard the threshold at each major energy marker of the Universal Story. These guardians are particularly skilled at sucking energy from you and pickpocketing your excitement for your project. Understand that you're being tested. Pursuing a creativity goal is not for the faint-hearted. And…how does one pass the test for admission into the next phase of your creativity? Simply and honestly recommit to your goals. Ultimately, only those who are committed to go the distance are ready to gain entry. Stand up to the threshold guardians.

Your spiritual pledge cites both your strengths and your weaknesses with an understanding that both are necessary in your evolution. What you believe about yourself is your ultimate way forward.

As you track your progress on the Universal Story, you begin to notice a pattern. You're attempting to replace procrastination with proactive acceptance of whatever form your creativity takes. The number of times each day you display a negative behavior shows up in the number of times you find it necessary to chant your affirmation. As you stand back to assess your progress, your stomach sinks. Rather than shrinking, the number of times your weakness plagues you has increased.

The realization that you're regressing rather than improving may cause you to fall into a depression. Before you allow yourself to slide completely into discouragement and give in to the urge to procrastinate, remind yourself that this is part of the process.

Life becomes difficult when your mind habits collide with change. Having dragged your feet in the past, it's not uncommon for your negative behavior to worsen now. Think of it as your mind having a temper tantrum in its desire to languish in the same old rut. Relapses are especially prevalent when you're under times of great stress and uncertainty. Rather than relent and fall back into your old patterns, repeat your mantra, persevere, and trust you are changing—every day, you're changing a little bit more.

Prove to the threshold guardians that you believe in yourself. Reject the belief that you're not good enough, not creative or imaginative or whatever else you currently mutter to yourself. Acknowledge your joy in witnessing your imagination becoming reality.

The threshold guardians nod. Entry to phase 3 is yours.

FIRST, BEFORE YOU CROSS OVER

Here at the threshold and before crossing into phase 3—Dive Deep—and the darker side of the Universal Story:

1. Take time to reevaluate your creativity goal and deadline. Weigh what you have accomplished. You now have a more realistic idea of how much time you need to enact the steps you've established. Remember, your deadline is an illusion of sorts—you can always change or ignore it. Used as a tool for discovery, deadlines create tension—will you reach your deadline or not? Emotions flair. How does the deadline affect your creativity?

2. Reorient your Universal Story and rearrange your steps according to where you are now and where you are headed. You're at the halfway point of the Universal Story. If there are any steps you have not yet accomplished in phase 2, move them to phase 3. Make the necessary changes to your Universal Story.

3. Look back through your answers in this workbook. If you left questions blank, are you able to answer them now? Without changing them, are any of your responses different now than what you recorded earlier in the programs?

4. Clean and tidy up your creativity space. Remove items that are uninspiring, and replace them with those that feed your spirit. Organize yourself.

RECOMMITMENT

This is a critical juncture where too many creatives falter and stall out. You've had a taste of what is required of you to make cards, block prints, or marble paper. Mesmerized by the sea breeze and hypnotized by the waves lapping against the boat, you may feel it easier just to quit. The damage to your spirit is incalculable if you do. And the truth is that quitting sets up a pattern that only makes the next time you arrive at this energy marker harder.

Similar to the exercise you did early in the program, ask yourself again: What have you started in the past and never finished—out of fear or simply because life got away from you? How did you feel about leaving behind something you had invested time and yourself in only to see it wither and die?

_____

_____

_____

_____

_____

What about now? Are you ready to recommit and cross over into phase 3—Dive Deep?

Yes   *No*

It's risky to follow the energy of your passion. As always, the choice to dive deeper into the Universal Story represents a leap of faith and a belief in the voyage's potential for growth.

The longer you dally at major thresholds, the longer it takes you to achieve your dreams and desires. As you teeter between what you have been doing and what you imagine comes next, thrust yourself forward. Always conspiring to assist you, the Universal Story is there to catch you. You are never alone.

The jewel in the Universal Story lies at the end. Seize this moment. Encourage, urge, and love yourself into moving forward. Walk through your fear.

TAKE ACTION

As you performed at the end of phase 1, ready to sail into the Sea of Creativity, again let the power of ritual be your guide as you sail into Dive Deep. This time, create your own ceremony. I heard from a creative asking for a poem or prayer to integrate into her symbolic crossing. Rather than turn to someone else's creativity, use your own imagination. Make this moment significant by creating a recommitment ritual expressly your own.

Then, close your eyes. Breathe. Review all you have accomplished and learned about your craft and yourself. Take another breath.

Ready?

Take the plunge…

PHASE 3

Dive
Deep

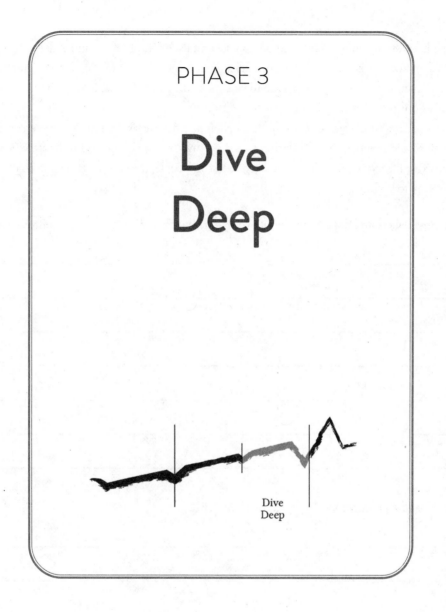

Dive
Deep

Your self-exploration, recommitment, and all you accomplished in phases 1 and 2 deem you ready. The gatekeepers step away. A submarine canyon cracks open to phase 3: Dive Deep. Don't mind the murky water and rough current. Poor conditions are to be expected. A storm brews in the north. Welcome to the dark middle of our program…

By now, you're painfully aware of old, useless beliefs and destructive habits. You haven't yet fully mastered the values and practices helpful during this deep dive of our voyage and ultimately needed to live your best creative life. Now you're suspended between two people, the *you* you're letting go of and the *you* it is your destiny to become.

List old, useless beliefs and destructive habits your spiritual mantra is helping you eliminate.

_____

_____

_____

_____

_____

_____

List new values and practices you're replacing them with.

_____

_____

_____

_____

_____

_____

The creative process is similar to every other relationship in your life. You start with stars in your eyes and can't stop thinking about the next step you plan to take. You want to spend all your time together. Then come squabbles and rows. Your eyes clear as you begin to understand how much patience and acceptance, compromise and dedication is required of you to make this relationship work.

Note how, in phase 3 of the Universal Story, the energy steadily rises to a peak of intensity. This illustrates how, from now on, each step toward your creativity goal and the lessons you're learning about yourself grow more difficult. Conflict and dark emotions are keynotes as you become more and more conscious of how the weight you've given the past drags you down and squashes your enthusiasm. The layers you're peeling back seem to be multiplying. Some days, for no reason, your creativity gives you the cold shoulder. You wonder if the effort is worth it.

When it comes to creating lately, where are you on the energy scale?

Enthusiastic   *Motivated*   *Relaxed*   *Lethargic*   *Apathetic*

BEWARE!

The resistance you met earlier in the program is nothing compared to the struggle you experience in phase 3. Your relationship with your creativity and your endurance will be tested in ways you can't even imagine. A firm grasp of the significance this phase of the Universal Story plays in your life and creativity grants you a sense of grace in the middle of chaos.

The dark middle reveals a world more wondrous and profound than you imagine. And though the passage is also more deeply painful and difficult than you anticipate, never doubt your love for your creativity goal. Growing pains aggravate your transition to an experienced and long-term relationship with your best creative life.

Isolation and Creativity

Water is an ancient symbol for the creative forces in your life. By now, you've traveled deep into your creativity goal and are making steady progress. Creating something out of your imagination is not a concept in your head—abstract and separate from who you are—but comes from the heart of you, your spirit. As such, creativity is an inner experience that typically demands a concentrated focus from a core of inner stillness and must be done alone.

The more passionate you are about what you're doing, the more the world drops away. You're physically alone. Far from lonely, immersed in the flow of creativity, you're intimately connected to your artistic expression.

Are you nodding, true for you? Or are you shaking your head, not true for you?

True   *Not true*

The paradigm I just described is truer for some creatives than for others. Those who value a quiet reflective life and are most comfortable in their own company thrive in the solitude that promotes innovation. But you may be more like a talented sculptor I worked with. As fantastic as her work was, she had an equally fantastic singing voice and would break into song at the slightest provocation with no qualms about jumping on a tabletop and belting out a show tune. She was always the life of the party with a laugh that could be heard from across a crowded room. Yet put her in a studio alone, and before long, her skin would start to crawl, and she'd be up and prowling the room like a caged lioness.

Circle what's true for you.

You love spending time alone.   Yes   *No*

You struggle with being alone.   Yes   *No*

TEMPERAMENT

Each of us is born with a fundamental temperament. Our inborn nature is instrumental in the development of our personality, which, in contrast, is learned and acquired over time. Our temperament affects our behavior and our emotions.

Awareness of your temperament gives you broader insight into your strengths and weaknesses when it comes to creating. Even more importantly, it helps you better understand when, where, and how you draw energy. Though there are other types of temperaments, here we focus on introverts and extroverts.

Extroverts

If you're born with a socially active temperament, you draw energy and inspiration from the company of others. Extroverts typically have busy lives engaged in all sorts of activities that involve family and community. If you fit the extroverted description, you may feel like your imagination goes off like fireworks, bursting with possibilities and making it hard for you to settle down.

Extroverts, not surprisingly, often grapple with creating alone. Many of the major trials and tests you undergo as an extrovert to live your best creative life revolve around coping with the isolation of creating alone.

Though extroverts may squirm at having to spend time alone, you can take heart when it's time to put your work out into the world. Then, you'll be in your strength.

Do you identify with the extrovert description?   *Yes*   *No*

In which ways?

COPING STRATEGIES FOR EXTROVERTS

If the extrovert description fits you, enlist someone to work with, make creativity dates where you work side-by-side, take breaks to encourage each other, and get back to work. Collaborate on a project or take a class. Work outside or in a library or café surrounded by others.

If your mind and imagination open through interacting with other creatives, you likely benefit from attending conferences, asking questions, and networking. A note of caution: as you fill your free time with activities associated with your creative passion, like discussing and exchanging views, be sure to schedule time to actually create.

Following are some ways extroverted creatives cope with creating alone.

"I have a writing buddy, and we discuss ideas."

"I stay connected to supportive people from all over the world through the internet."

"It's hard to sit for hours on end. I have to move around and expose myself to outside influences to feel inspired."

Extroverts thrive in stimulating environments—in crowded coffee shops and writing grottos, on public blogs, and in critique groups, online chat rooms, and writing platforms. You enjoy the social aspect of brainstorming and end up entertaining many more ideas than you may have done alone.

LIKE A PRETZEL

As I mentioned earlier in the program, be careful about sharing your work too early with others.

"I'm way too susceptible to bending myself like a pretzel when I hear suggestions. I need to be strong in myself first."

I recommend keeping your creativity confidential and any conversation around it low-key at first. Not because you're scared, but because you're nurturing a slender and fragile opening of your spirit. This is true for all mediums of creative expression—wait until you've shaped your work to the best of your ability. That way, you have a clear sense of your vision before others begin sharing their impressions with you.

Are you able to keep your work to yourself until you're finished before showing it to anyone else?

Yes   No

If no, what are you hoping to gain by showing your work early?

_____

_____

_____

_____

_____

_____

As an extrovert, waiting may be excruciating to you. You're in the flow and you want to show off your efforts to anyone who will listen. Rest assured that if you can hold off, each brilliant step forward you take is noticed. Deep down your spirit sees, hears, and tastes your accomplishments, and is pleased and strengthened.

Introverts

Not everyone is designed to be so publically out there. If you're born with the temperament of introversion, you're reflective and reserved. You're more comfortable in the company of a few than many. You tend to thrive in a calm, quiet environment without many distractions. A creative with an introvert's temperament prefers to be alone. Unlike an extroverted creative, who loses energy in solitude, an introvert draws energy in solitude.

What becomes vitally important to introverted creatives is having a safe space to be still, where you're wrapped in things you love and that inspire your imagination, a place where your creativity can flow.

You thrive in the isolation of creating alone, but when you reach the final phase of the program, and it's time to put your work out into the world, you may wish to gain tips from your more extroverted friends.

Do you identify with the introvert description?   *Yes*   *No*

In which ways?

_____

_____

_____

_____

_____

_____

Tendency

Explore your introverted and extrovert tendencies for a better understanding of your process. The deeper you dive into the Universal Story, whatever you struggle with now is only going to worsen until you relax and accept the present moment. You may wish to refine and rewrite your spiritual pledge to incorporate what you now perceive as strengths and weaknesses based on your temperament and with an awareness of how you feel creating alone.

Write your revised spiritual mantra here.

_____

_____

_____

Your pledge or mantra is intended to bring you back to yourself as you acknowledge what typically blocks you. You're reminded of what you're good at. You're attempting to replace a negative trait, emotion, or belief with strength. In other words, you're replacing counterproductive mind habits with positive ones. If you revel in alone time, include that as your strength in your pledge. Visualize yourself acting in your strength. Listen to your spirit's inner wisdom. Feel your fear dissolve and your sadness reconnect to happiness. Continue to discover, acknowledge, and nurture your strengths.

Moments when you're innovating are opportunities to wake up to your inner self. Don't judge what you find. Jot down both when your energy soars and you feel rejuvenated and when difficulties arise. You are beginning to understand what your mind habits are doing to your energy and belief in yourself. Some habits make you want to give up. Other beliefs urge you forward.

What are you learning about your creative impulses? List beliefs, strategies, feelings, and habits that draw you to create.

_____

_____

_____

_____

_____

_____

List beliefs, strategies, feelings, and habits that spin you away from wanting to create.

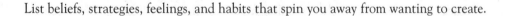

_____

_____

_____

_____

_____

_____

PHYSICAL VERSUS SPIRITUAL ISOLATION

Embrace your temperament and, when necessary, also compensate for it. Understanding your temperament requires practice, showing up, and trying different approaches until you find what works for you.

Whether an extrovert or introvert, you ultimately have to learn to create alone. Yes, extroverts may choose to write with others. Still, they enter their imagination alone. Often, introverts have been bullied or enticed into disowning their very nature in favor of becoming more outgoing and social. If that's your case, you may have to actually relearn how to be comfortable with being alone again.

How are you with handling the alone part of a creative life? (1 = you hate it and you're not coping well versus 10 = you love it; it's your favorite part)

1   2   3   4   5   6   7   8   9   10

What we're talking about here is physical isolation versus spiritual isolation. You may separate yourself physically to create. Always cleave to your spirit. The better you know yourself, the better able you are to connect with your inner world. Solitude and isolation and inner stillness are replenishing to the spirit. Nothing feeds your spirit as well as living your best creative life.

Alone versus Lonely

Lots of us experience bouts of loneliness that stem less from creating alone; it's more like a general unease, low-grade depression, lack of energy, and feeling lonely even in a group of people. Don't run from your emotions. Deny them, and you're apt to become resentful and bitter. Allow yourself to fully feel.

Whom do you feel comfortable reaching out to when you're feeling lonely?

_____

_____

_____

_____

When you're feeling lonely, how easy is it for you to reach out and connect with someone? (1 = impossible to 10 = effortless)

1   2   3   4   5   6   7   8   9   10

Uncertainty and insecurity about what you're doing create a sense of loneliness. You doubt yourself and feel alone, separate and different from the flow of humanity around you. Isolated, your creativity goes into hiding.

Loneliness is an absence of affection that stems from sadness, which is the loss of control over a source of love or attention. In other words, you want something, and you feel you can't have it.

Right now, without thinking, jot down what you really want.

_____

_____

_____

_____

_____

Do you believe you can have what you really want?   *Yes*   *No*

If no, what needs to change?

_____

_____

_____

_____

Each time uncertainty, pain, loneliness, and isolation overtake you is a test. You will often want to run from the test. Ignore it. Walk away. Turn your back. Call for help. Tomorrow the test still waits. And the next day and the next, until you finally give up the resistance, stick with the discomfort, hang in there with the loneliness, accept the isolation, and create. With your white flag of surrender come gifts of inspiration, energy, and acceptance.

When you want to wait until you feel better, you're inspired, the house is spotless, or the noise is gone, but instead you stay and practice even in the worst situation, you're moving ever nearer to the heart of creativity.

What do you need in order to create? List internal and external needs you have to create.

_____

_____

_____

_____

_____

_____

_____

Next...cross out each need you listed.

Do this whenever you hear yourself give an excuse for why you're not showing up for your creativity. Write the excuse. And then...cross it out.

_____

_____

_____

_____

_____

_____

_____

_____

_____

Your Wild Spirit

When you stop holding back with excuses, are willing to put everything out on the kitchen table—the good, the imperfect, and the ugly—and keep creating no matter what your environment or circumstances, only then do you begin to express your truth. Until you willingly forfeit all your needs—company or quiet, your internal critic, to be right, perfection, pain and heartache, inspiration, or support—only then do you gain access to the miraculous and your wild spirit.

Lose yourself in your art. Slowly, loneliness and the feeling of being cut off and separated from all you know and love transform into a feeling of oneness with the world and even the universe. And then, you're good to just…be. You begin to feel something real inside, intangible and miraculous even. You honor your actions in service of creativity.

Value in Every Attempt

Next time you rush to delete a horribly written scene, clean up the mess of a ruined pot, and do whatever you can to hide evidence of your less-than-perfect attempt, instead allow yourself time to face what you tried that failed to live up to your expectations. Open your heart. Rest your thoughts, and feel what you're feeling. There is value in every attempt—a message, a lesson, wisdom, a gift, a spark of genius. Learn to love the challenges and failures as much as the ease and successes.

Living a creative life is challenging and messy and rocky. When you attempt to do everything you can to avoid or lessen the challenges, you're missing the point of creating. Living your best creative life means taking risks, facing the unknown, accepting the tests, and admitting your imperfections. If you're not, you're not creating fully awake.

When you play by the rules of your culture and comply with what others decide is right, you seldom touch your truth. When conventional expectations control your actions, breaking rules, throwing off constraints, and freeing yourself take inner strength and conviction.

There are those who appear to have it all together and life figured out. Good for them! We all deserve to shimmy and whoop and holler and throw our fists in the air to celebrate our successes and those times we're in the creative flow toward our goals. Then, at some point when you're ready to continue reaching and stretching and risking everything in your quest to find your strengths and discover who you truly are, step out in mid-air…see what happens next.

TAKE ACTION

Study your Universal Story. Evaluate the steps you've accomplished and those left to be done.

Measure your use of your spiritual pledge and those times you detached from the uncertainty of your creative project and plugged into the Universal Story's promise of transformation. Fill in any missing steps toward reaching your creativity. Add short-term goals that delight you. The clearer your vision of your creative piece, yourself at your best, and your ideal environment, the more open and certain the energy around you.

A perfectly formed idea for the next step toward your outer creativity goal enters your mind. Excitement builds. Solitude and isolation dissolve into irrelevant concepts as you're off and creating fully in the flow and connected to your expression.

Record how far along you are with your external goal.

_____

_____

_____

_____

Write a couple of sentences or draw a stick figure of how you're feeling about what you've accomplished.

_____

_____

_____

_____

STEP 12

Motivation

Way back in the beginning of the program, you identified dreams and desires that you then crafted into a creativity goal. We started with what you most yearn for because the more willing and determined you are to reach your goal, the greater your motivation to keep at it all the way to the end. Boundless creativity demands strong motivation because, as you've already experienced, the deeper you dive into your creativity, the more intense the obstacles.

A sense of purpose, along with personal incentives, motivates you to persevere. Motivation is your reason for doing what you set out to do, especially when all appears lost. Your motivation mirrors your passion for what you're doing.

Often, the motivation that got you started at the beginning of a creative project may not be enough to keep you going as the going gets harder and you become more emotional. Weak motivation fails to inspire your commitment through such a challenging voyage.

Take note on the Universal Story how we're moving ever nearer to the highest point energetically so far. This ascent reflects energy rising as disappointment and setbacks and frustrations multiply. Sure, what you first envisioned caused you to act and initiate change. Now, you may feel urged to think expansively and dramatically to find a more substantial, more universal, and emotionally connective motivation to keep you going.

First, rewrite your creativity goal.

_____

_____

_____

_____

Is this the same goal you started the program with? Circle your answer.   *Yes*   *No*

If you answered no, why did you change your goal, and have you changed it more than once?

_____

_____

_____

_____

Next, attempt to think back to the beginning of the program and write down what motivated you to choose the creativity goal that you did and what your reason(s) for taking action were.

_____

_____

_____

_____

Now, ask yourself if your initial motivation is strong enough to sustain you even during the darkest times. Circle your answer.

Yes   No

If you wrote no, before you reconsider your motivation, first let's discuss two kinds of motivation.

EXTRINSIC MOTIVATION

Extrinsic motivation is any reason that arises from outside of your essential nature for why you're doing what you're doing. Motivation originating from outside of you has little to do with your spirit. Rather, it is driven by external rewards like fame, money, approval, grades, social recognition, validation, "I'll show you," prestige, honor, revenge, praise, or the need to prove yourself to someone or something other than you.

In a recent survey, I asked writers and artists what motivates them to show up for their creativity. Following are some of the extrinsic motivations expressed.

"I want to make enough money with my art so I can quit my day job."

"I'm motivated by the recognition I hope to get."

"I'm a member of a group that makes me accountable."

What motivates you extrinsically to show up for your creativity?

_____

_____

_____

_____

_____

Extrinsic motivation is often driven by the ego; you want to demonstrate your ability and achievement in comparison to business partners, family, those who doubt you, or your friends. You may enjoy what you're doing, but that pleasure is not what drives you to achieve an outstanding performance. Motivation that comes from outside of you often results from measuring your success by the grades you receive in the school, the acceptance of those you care about, the all-mighty pursuit of money, or wanting to keep up with those you admire.

Extrinsic motivation can be powerful and very effective, especially so for tasks that do not require the type of creativity that demands you dive deep enough to bypass the mundane and all you have learned to access innovation from your deeper wisdom and touch your inner truth.

To live your best creative life asks that you stop being in service to others, at least not primarily, but in service to your art.

INTRINSIC MOTIVATION

Intrinsic motivation arises from inside of you as a deep inner stirring and ancient urging. Motivated by curiosity to see what you can do, inner motivation belongs to you and you alone. The reasons you take on your creativity project and show up daily for your art are essential to your being. This sort of motivation is inseparable from you and is deeply satisfying at a core or spiritual level.

From the same survey about what motivates creatives to show up for their creativity, the following are examples of intrinsic motivation.

"Creativity brings a calmness to my hectic world, so motivation is easy."

"I usually give myself a pep talk. I say things like, 'that bit of housework that you think needs to be done right now can wait for one hour' or 'you'll feel more energetic after you paint for awhile.' "

"I create to escape the cares of the world."

What drives you intrinsically to show up for your creativity?

_____

_____

_____

_____

We're not always in touch with intrinsic motivation, because the prevailing culture places more value on material success than spiritual wisdom. Yet to access boundless creativity, first you have to unshackle yourself from convention, liberate yourself from the status quo, release yourself from what others think, and remain open to what's going on inside of you.

WHAT YOU STAND TO LOSE

Another way to find out what motivates you to keep creating even when you don't much feel like it is to ask what you stand to lose if not successful.

"My dream."

"My self-esteem."

"A happy life."

"My life's purpose."

These sorts of responses help ensure you'll keep at your goal even when faced with possible failure. Problems arise when you tell yourself, as one creative put it:

"It's not that big of a deal if I keep going or I stop."

If you lose nothing by not reaching your creativity goal, you may not have enough motivation to encourage yourself when times are hard and all the external motivation dwindles…not enough right now, anyway. This all changes once you stop looking outside yourself, and you appreciate that creativity connects you to your spirit and all that it brings to your life.

What do you stand to lose if you don't complete your creativity goal?

_____

_____

_____

_____

Reconsider your motivation. Circle whether you believe you're motivated intrinsically, extrinsically, or both.

Intrinsic   *Extrinsic*   *Both*

What is motivating you to complete this program?

_____

_____

_____

_____

Now, what motivates you to complete your creativity goal?

_____

_____

_____

_____

Consideration

Perhaps you were externally motivated when you set out on this voyage. Many creatives turn to art in hopes of making a living with their writing or painting or designs or music. As the truth sets in that to quit your day job actually takes a good deal more than talent alone, this motivation typically fades. When this happens, turn first to your spiritual pledge. The daily repetition of your affirmation stimulates positive, upbeat energy and boosts your enthusiasm to create.

Next, if you started motivated by things outside yourself, take a moment to search inward. By now, you've spent time with your art, dealt with the aloneness required, felt the well-being when in the flow of creativity, and perhaps even accessed a place you didn't know was waiting inside, a place where the outer world vanishes and time stands still.

List what internal incentives might help pull you up when you falter.

_____

_____

_____

_____

Or, if you started motivated internally, consider adding external motivation. Include steps at the end of your Universal Story to enter your completed work in a contest or apply for a grant.

List what external incentives might help pull you up when you falter.

_____

_____

_____

_____

The steps you've completed are helping you to form a productive habit and a positive self-image and to practice acceptance, all of which are especially important as the challenges increase in number and intensity.

Explore what you've felt and learned as you've taken the early steps toward your goal. Record the internal rewards you've gained through your art.

_____

_____

_____

_____

_____

If you've been creating or attempting to create before now, what is the earliest inspiration you remember and the first to motivate you?

_____

_____

_____

_____

_____

STICKING TO YOUR PLAN

Whether you're motivated by things outside of you or internally motivated, I ask you to stick to the plan, at least this time through. By reaching your goal, you complete what you set out to do, and you prove you're trustworthy. Consistency creates habits and routines. Each time you create repeatedly with purpose, intention, and emphasis, the practice enters the realm of a ritual.

Even more importantly, you fulfill a commitment to yourself. By staying true to yourself, you strengthen a belief in yourself. Conversely, by not honoring promises to yourself, you slowly erode trust in yourself. And you can do actual harm to your spirit. That's why it's best not to promise to do something you know you won't keep. Or, perhaps, you do everything you can to stay true to your promises to others while easily breaking personal promises and ultimately letting yourself down. Completing this program and achieving your creativity goal are opportunities to prove to your spirit that you're reliable and have your best interests at heart.

If you hear yourself saying to yourself or to others, *it's just a little goal I'm trying out*, you're hedging your bet. That way, if you fail to finish or what you create isn't very good, you can always fall back on your indifference, your feeling that it wasn't a big deal to begin with. Dismissing your creativity with *oh, it's nothing* or *it's not important* is a form of self-negation and trivializes your spirit. When you put yourself in any position other than the primary one, you end up discrediting your innate gifts.

No Turning Back

Don't be surprised when lately you find yourself fighting fatigue. Or you feel a pang of nostalgia for your favorite shows, but you gave away your television. Even as your creative vision every day becomes clearer and more real to you, when you glance at the steps left to do, the demands piling up, and how far you still have to go before you reach your deadline, it's not uncommon for your enthusiasm to wilt. The energy of the Universal Story steadily rises ever higher as you find yourself backsliding.

You appreciate the discipline you're learning by staying true to the schedule you created, but having to show up is starting to pale compared to the good old lazy days of goofing off with your friends, shopping, and spending time together. The only thing keeping you going is the recommitment you made at the end of phase 2.

Check which of the following is true for you:

☐ I'm energized following the steps I plotted for my creativity goal and learning about myself.

☐ I'm worried about making it to the end and what it means if I fail.

If you're energized, keep going strong! If you're faltering, you're not alone. Though what you're feeling is normal, rather than give in to your old ways and run the other way, focus on your feelings. Attempt to *be* with them. Feel them. Then write about them. Dance about them. They're part of the creative life. Don't hide from them. Don't blame and feel guilty. This is yet another test, and tests always come with gifts.

Our first impulse is to quit when the going gets rough. Write about a time in your past when you wanted to quit and didn't.

What gift were you awarded for your perseverance?

_____

_____

_____

Stay True to Yourself

Does your goal feel within reach?   *Yes*   *No*

The point of the work you're doing is to birth a new life filled with freshness and vibrancy. Along with the creative practice you gain, new skills you're developing, lessons you're learning, and strength you're building, there is a deeper meaning behind the trials you face. Are you willing to do whatever is required to break down the past and create a future in your image? To strive toward the person you're uniquely meant to be and learn to trust and respect yourself and rely on your heart and your spirit's wisdom takes time and dedication. Insight into the Universal Story prepares you with an awareness of what's coming.

Awaken Further

Each sticky note you accomplish on the Universal Story advances you toward your long-term goal. Each day brings you yet another day nearer to your deadline. Each time you catch yourself before falling prey to your internal opposition, feel it, and then replace it with a chant of your highest self, you awaken further. When your oath sinks to an intimate level, you activate new dimensions into creativity. Rather than being gripped by old thinking, you remember to consider the positive. You become enlivened and fortified deep in the moment of creating and having fun. Your creativity flourishes.

To move from the unconscious roles you embody to freedom demands a full acceptance and integration of all parts of you. And—this is huge—you are doing just that. More and more you're becoming conscious of your usual thoughts and beliefs as they take over your mind. You may still be led by old thinking, but when you know you are, the hold it has over you weakens, and you begin to break free.

You're becoming more independent of others' holds on you as you assume authority over your own life. In so doing, you repossess the personal power you've surrendered to outside forces. Then, you use this power to accomplish your short-term creativity steps.

If, on the other hand, you're struggling to stay accountable to yourself and not accomplishing your short-term steps, consider enlisting a supportive ally who will hold you accountable. Choose someone who will check in with you periodically to ask you about your progress and then lovingly listen without giving advice. Take note of the excuses you make.

_____

_____

_____

What You Don't Know

This dark phase of the Universal Story is meant to challenge your weaknesses and beliefs and emotions. The energy grows more intense with each passing day, as reflected in the mounting difficulties you face. We often don't know why at the time, yet the information, knowledge, and practice you gain here is critical for what you'll confront in phase 4. The pushback you currently experience may not be easy, but as you master your emotions, what you learn brings immense benefits as your actions and words set the stage for your best creative life.

Are you surprised you've stuck with your project this long?   *Yes*   *No*

How do you traditionally react when faced with hard times and challenges?

_____

_____

_____

_____

_____

_____

_____

Gather together your intrinsic and extrinsic motivation and any incentives you can dream up, because you're quickly going to need all the support you can get. Hold tight to your belief in the transformational power of the Universal Story. What comes next has the potential to break your heart.

TAKE ACTION

Stand in front of your Universal Story. Acknowledge how far along you are toward your goal. Celebrate your accomplishments. Then, for the next seven days, complete each step at the same time and same place.

Check off the days you're successful.

- ☐ Monday

- ☐ Tuesday

- ☐ Wednesday

- ☐ Thursday

- ☐ Friday

- ☐ Saturday

- ☐ Sunday

STEP 13

Dark Emotions, Blocks, and the Death of Your Vision

Your artistic vision crystalizes with each step you complete on your Universal Story toward your creativity goal. Thanks to the help of your spiritual pledge, tracking your emotions on the emotion trees, and diving deep to link the past with your emotions today, you're more in touch with your feelings. You've cut down the amount and severity of your anger when you lash out (fear). You continue to turn passive and retreat (sadness), only now you're aware of it and only sporadically run away. You still manipulate others (sadness and fear), but now you know enough to recognize what you're doing.

Then, one day, you awaken to a storm at sea. On deck, you're met with high winds and black clouds. Monster waves slam against the boat. Rather than outrun the storm, you seem to be heading straight into heavy rain. You run to check on the landscape you've been painting for weeks. As a jagged streak of lightning flashes, you suddenly notice only color and no unifying theme. Or the loads of words and scenes you generated don't add up to a story. Your song sounds beautiful but lacks vitality and feels apart from the truth you're exploring. You're writing a historical novel and suddenly are drowning in subplots and overrun with characters. Tangled in chaos and confusion and feeling a mess, you haven't the vaguest idea what your story is about anymore. You're learning your craft as you go and keep sensing that something essential is missing. What exactly that essential something is has you stumped, with no idea how to fix it.

Daily, and exponentially, your dismay builds as you find, like a pelican hunting at sea, you haven't plunged deep enough. You've been freely creating without any restrictions, structure, or a disciplined approach to your piece. Rather than venture far and independently, you've hugged social and cultural norms too tightly. The thought of editing and applying order and restraint to shape your piece into its true form feels beyond you. More and more, you seriously doubt you possess any talent at all. Dark emotions threaten your way forward. You lash out. You freeze up. You feel sick to your stomach.

DARK EMOTIONS

You hit a wall and believe you've failed. This perceived failure happens either through no fault of your own or because of self-sabotaging habits and beliefs. Failure happens when you unconsciously expect to fail, when you've wandered too far afield from your destiny, or when you've stumbled and fallen short of your promise. A sense of doom traditionally hits right about now on the Universal Story.

> *"I asked someone to read a manuscript and give his opinion. Even though I knew intellectually that it wasn't the kind of book he would normally read, his comments were extremely counterproductive. They made me doubt my ability to write. They set me back years."*

> *"A project I've worked on for years I still haven't completed, and it eats at me."*

> *"Seeing others succeed in ways I haven't makes me want to quit."*

The more intense the stakes, the darker the emotions you feel. Negative actions, reactions, and adverse thoughts stem from fear. Grief and withdrawal stem from sadness. This point is the prime testing ground and center of conflict, where all your sides are exposed.

Is your work bringing up any dark emotions in you?   *Yes*   *No*

If yes, write a bit about your experience.

_____

_____

_____

_____

_____

More and more, you're gripped with jealousy, resentment, bitterness, spitefulness, stubbornness, confusion, sorrow, fear, and weakness. The discovery of your more unpleasant sides creates yet more dark emotions. You know something has to change.

Write about a time—with either your current creativity goal or at some other point in your life—when you felt lost and overcome with dark emotions. Include what happened next.

_____

_____

_____

_____

_____

_____

Are you feeling any dark emotions right now?   *Yes*   *No*

If you answered yes, what thoughts are bringing on the dark emotions?

_____

_____

_____

_____

_____

CHANGE HAPPENS

This is also a time when you may begin dressing differently and in ways that better reflect your individuality and creativity. If you're a writer, you may find yourself wearing black. Artists don long flowy clothes. Potters throw on a thick apron. Iron artists prefer fireproof overalls. Your family and friends notice and start questioning what's going on, why the changes?

The more drastically altered your external appearance, the words you speak, and the schedules you keep, the more pushback you receive from people who represent your old world. As your art becomes more wild and edgy, it is more likely there will be those who reject you as a rule-breaker and even dangerous. Before long, you're branded an outsider.

Opening up to your creativity has turned you more sensitive. As a result, you're more reactive. As the divide grows between what's becoming more and more valuable to you and what's of little consequence to others, you begin moving away from friends you cherished in the past. They're either so caught up in their own lives that they're oblivious to the changes you're making in your life, or what you're doing and learning isn't of much interest to them, and they seldom ask about your project. You're restless and bored by conversations you used to actively engage in. No longer interested in the things you once were, you travel deeper and deeper into your own knowing. Yet you often feel lonely and confused. Lately, feelings of vulnerability, uncertainty, and insecurity are more aggressively interfering with your creativity.

Bereft

Because you're acting and thinking in new ways, you shine a mirror on other people's fears and limitations. Either your changes inspire others to change or they lash out at you or turn away.

Bereft both by your failure to adequately convey your vision and the lack of support, slowly or rapidly, your creativity dries up.

"I'm so blocked I've completely stopped writing, and I know it's due to negative thoughts and stress."

"I hit a dry spell and haven't gotten anything on the canvas for months."

"I've lost all hope and inspiration."

"I can't get past chapter 3."

We live in a culture steeped in scientific and medical pursuits over emotional and spiritual expression. Logic and objectivity are rewarded. Intuition and imagination are dismissed. Sentimentality is best kept under control, and all moods must be made agreeable. The patriarchal legacy passed down keeps emotions straitjacketed and medicated. You want to call out your friends and family. Instead, you hold in your feelings and, more and more, feel blocked.

Circle those with whom you feel comfortable honestly sharing your feelings.

Family   Old friends   New friends   Acquaintances   Strangers   Your journal

STAGNATION

Pressure mounts as you move ever nearer to your goal. The stakes of what you've taken on become more intense as antagonists internal, external, and embodied in the very project you've undertaken work harder and more rigorously to block your success. Blocks lead to stagnation. Rather than flowing, moving, and developing, your creativity and imagination languish. You understand how much you're losing—your old ways of behaving and thinking, old friends and old habits—to dive deeper and further into your creative life. You find yourself torn between who you were and who you're becoming.

It takes gumption to release the old and make friends with yourself, your spirit, and your creativity and believe in the path you've chosen. Instead, you fixate on the old ways of doing what you've always done and reacting how you've always reacted. You are hesitant to explore a new identity and the territory spread out before you. As you resist watching your old personality undergo a rapid or slow death, your imagination blocks.

Refusing to let the feeling of hitting a wall do you in, you're driven to prove to yourself you're not a loser. Buoyed by having progressed further with your writing than ever before, you take action. Your creativity goal includes a method to measure success: submit your first chapter to a literary contest or a critique group, post it online, query an agent, or read a chapter at your local bookstore's open mike night.

"People are really going to dig my work."

You begin a few of the measurable steps you plotted at the end of the Universal Story now, well before you've completed your vision. Though you know showing your work this early on is risky, you're confident in your new skills and believe you can handle whatever comes.

In less than a week, you receive rejection letters—all of them with the anonymous salutation "Dear author"—from all five agents, your grant application wasn't received and this year's deadline has passed, overnight you lose fifty Instagram followers, you suffer through an excoriating critique of your first chapter. Fears and regrets boil to the surface. Completely overwhelmed, you know you're not strong enough, good enough, or worthy enough to succeed.

And now, even after all the work you've done and insight gained, the limb you are clutching, suspended over a gorge, cracks. There is no safety net.

Whom can you reach out to when you're falling apart?

_____

_____

_____

When was the last time you reached out to this person?

_____

_____

_____

How about an encouraging check-in now?   *Yes*   *No*

DEATH OF YOUR VISION

THE UNIVERSAL STORY

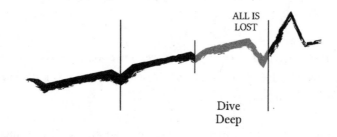

Having all your powers tested while experiencing any form of negativity—internal or external or both at the same time—is tough. Shoved at the end of a long onslaught of challenges—putting yourself and your art first, learning how to create shadows in your paintings, overcoming your fear of the forge, believing in yourself—proves too much. Self-doubt transmutes into an uncontrollable monster. Your spiritual mantra is much too puny and ineffective to offer the life support you require now. Unprepared, you suffer a crisis in the depths of a very dark night; all appears lost.

Dark emotions, blocks, and stagnation are all symptoms of the third and most deadly energy marker—All Is Lost, the Crisis, Dark Night, or Black Moment—seen where the rising energy on the Universal Story reaches the highest peak so far. Often, failure, brokenness, fear, emptiness, alienation, and great loss—your ego destroyed—leave room for profound growth. In every endeavor, obstacles multiply to a breaking point that signifies the death of your creative vision and dream, and even your nerve.

The intensifying energy explodes, spewing out all vestiges of negativity imprisoned inside and holding you back. The degree of rupture is directly related to how hidden your dark side has been and is often fed by a primary fear related to an earlier wound that splintered you from standing on your own.

- *Explosion.* Externally, everything shakes. Glass shatters. The kiln explodes. Your computer crashes. Frying oil for your experimental recipe sets off a kitchen fire. Your design falls flat. People walk out on your performance. Your ego is crushed.

- *Implosion.* Internally, everything rocks. Your heart bleeds. Your vision vaporizes. Your work shrivels. Your enthusiasm and belief in yourself spoil. Your confidence dies. Your spirit is crushed.

At the Dark Night, typically, everything that can go wrong does. Like a tight set of waves, one disaster crashes as the next one crests. Hopelessness, as all appears lost, is not the final struggle on your way to success. It is, however, the most defining moment of your entire life.

Catastrophic

A moment as catastrophic as this occurs on such a universal level because to ultimately transform and gain wisdom, break from your ego, and truly connect to your spirit involves a magnificent struggle. An inability to translate the depths of creativity creates chaos and confusion as you usher your inner life out into the light.

Though bringing memories up from the dead or wherever you keep your deepest secrets hidden is painful, take a moment to consider and record a breakdown or crisis or dark night you've experienced in the past, a time when you lost meaning in your life.

Describe an all-is-lost moment that was directly related to your creativity or something else entirely.

_____

_____

_____

_____

_____

_____

"Two weeks after my first book was released, my son died. Now I'm always scared something else horrible will happen."

"I showed people my ragged first draft, and what happened next put me off writing."

"I lost my ability to paint due to a double shoulder injury. I had a lot of my self-esteem and joy tied up in the artistic part of my career, and I wondered who I was, if not a painter. Finances suffered, I went through my savings, and I handled it poorly. I lost my confidence. I became paralyzed with fear that my best years were behind me."

You're in a transition of identity. You may have heard the age-old expression, *you have to lose yourself to find yourself.* For our purposes here, it may be more apt to say, *you have to lose your vision to find your true vision.* You find yourself questioning if your project has meaning, purpose, importance, or value. *What am I trying to do, say, convey? Does it matter?* When you begin to wrestle with these big questions, you've entered the Dark Night.

Often, the disaster is severe enough to send you to your knees. This breakdown will ultimately lead to a breakthrough, but first you have to die to who you've always been. Death leads the way to recreation and new birth. Though old ways of believing, doing things, and thinking served you in the past, now they limit you and must be destroyed.

"I consistently can't come up with good endings to my stories, which makes me believe I'm not good enough, so I stopped writing."

"My dad was my biggest believer. His death stopped me cold."

"My trusted editor said in response to what I've been working on for years something like, 'this isn't just bad, it's really terrible, just unbelievably bad.' I still wrestle with it and have yet to rebound."

What has the power to send you to your knees and rob you of your nerve?

_____

_____

_____

_____

_____

Without undergoing a major breakdown, if you sail effortlessly to success, all that changes is your outer life. Your inner life receives little lasting benefit. Or, as some creatives admit, when they say they haven't had any major setbacks, they haven't really pushed themselves or their work.

"In large part because I haven't put myself in any particularly vulnerable positions."

Risk-Taker

By taking risks, you're preforming an act of alchemy. Alchemy is a ritual of subjecting base metals (the imperfect individual) to scorching fire (challenges and change), burning off the dross (burdens and flaws) and transforming them into gold (the fully realized individual). Alchemy is the seemingly miraculous power or process of change in form, appearance, or nature at depth and over time that produces your inner gold.

Heat in the form of outer and inner obstacles and resistance sends the energy blazing ever hotter. Metaphorically, you're burning off the dross in preparation for full transformation.

Never fear, as devastating as all this may be, it is part of the process and necessary to experience in readiness for the next step in our voyage. You observe where you currently stand on the Universal Story with new eyes. Defeat happens. Only you have the authority over how you emotionally respond.

TAKE ACTION

Draft a new affirmation with the power to override your fears and insecurities and to encourage you to keep going. You better understand the deeper meaning of the voyage now. Accept the idea of failure, keep chanting, and walk into the fire.

Write your new affirmation here.

_____

_____

_____

_____

STEP 14

The Abyss and Emotional Wounds

THE UNIVERSAL STORY

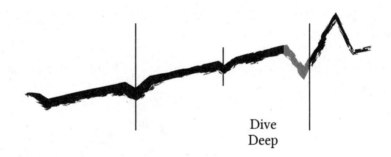

Dive
Deep

At this all-is-lost moment in the Universal Story, the boat pitches, slinging you into the water in the shadows of a harsh rock formation jutting from the sea. Heavy-hearted, hopeless, and paranoid, you clutch at the cliffs, unable to stop your slide into a pitch-black hole. You crumble at the bottom, your hands bloody and knuckles torn. The steep decline in the Universal Story symbolizes the abyss that comes after a crisis. This fall from grace leaves you all alone, empty, stripped of everything, and overcome with despair.

This is a creative life-*and*-death moment, one to see all the way through to the other side. Believing you're doomed and unable to succeed at your art leaves you feeling a victim. Sometimes this feeling can last for a lifetime…but when you endure the abyss and journey through it, you arise liberated and renewed.

It's as if you've been waiting your whole life for the other shoe to drop. Then, unexpectedly, you notice you're not alone. Your eyes adjust to the darkness, and you hear spirit-broken zombies mutter while the all-together-dead skirt around you. You are joined with others in loss.

Following the Universal Story's first peak, you are forced to slide inward. All you can do is breathe. Become aware of what you're feeling and saying to yourself.

Relax and explore when you felt this way before. Did you allow yourself to descend into darkness, or did you avoid and distract?

_____

_____

_____

_____

Decide to do things differently this time. Sort out what happened. Nurse your wounds. Search for messages, meaning, and signs.

Do you make a habit of pushing aside and ignoring unpleasant feelings, or do you face your emotions and try to understand them?

Ignore   *Explore*

FERTILE GROUND

Whether causing grave damage or even threatening your life, the role of a crisis is to force you to face yourself, and thus it acts as a cathartic release. Rather than panic, shut down, lash out, or struggle to get everything back to your old, predictable way of thinking and acting, face the feelings that control you. Be open. Trust that this crisis is an opportunity to reclaim the power you surrendered. As you feel, observe yourself caught up in scared and hurt feelings. The pit of the abyss is a wasteland of released tension and anxiety from feelings and memories repressed for years. It's also fertile ground for purification and expansion. The abyss is sacred space where true healing begins.

At first glance, the abyss may appear the antithesis of sacred, as it is cast in shadows and populated with sleepwalkers and ghosts. Search the diffused energy for answers. This lowest point energetically in the entire Universal Story determines how you spend the next few days, weeks, years—a lifetime. Will you be awake or wounded?

The low point of your voyage is a time of death (literal or the death of an illusion or old personality). Lacking defensive postures, you lose everything. If you haven't learned endurance, perseverance, boundaries, acceptance, patience, compassion, and forgiveness, you're forced to engage them now. The downward line indicates an emotional limbo that, if you're not careful, becomes a trap.

If you suffered the loss of everything, what would you miss the most?

_____

_____

_____

_____

_____

_____

_____

BACKSTORY WOUND

Crises strike in varying degrees of magnitude. Some dark nights are serious enough to be the emotional center of your life. Devastating feedback and unfortunate events in your creativity project have the potential to awaken the jaws of phantom pain and reveal a giant seeping wound.

This old injury is known as your backstory wound. Your everyday life is your front story. Your backstory is everything that happened before the present moment. A backstory wound is something in your past that robbed you of your self-respect and belief in yourself. As a result, you handed some or all your authority and power over to failure. You traded happiness and joy for chronic fear and cynicism.

Nearly everyone has an ancient story seared in their memory with details, as if it's happening right now in real time. This previous trauma, disappointment, betrayal, deception, humiliation, pain, hurt, or bullying in your past—near past or distant—destroyed your original state of perfection, minimized your abilities, and continues to haunt you today. Violence, neglect, or abandonment breaks your spirit. Someone did you wrong and has to pay. So, let me ask you. How come you're the one living half a life of negative secondary emotions and dark energy?

You create stories in your mind about your relationship to life. You become so entangled in the stories that every time you repeat your version, you relive the original flood of emotions until they're always right beneath the surface of your skin in your present-day life—anxiety, fear, nightmares, phobias, depression, grief, flashbacks, mistrust, and isolation. Reliving stories becomes an addiction; it's easier than coming up with an entirely new story. Often, disaster strikes from live emotions fixed in your stories.

Look back on the common themes of loss and trauma from your past. What is the story by which you define your creative life?

Coping Mechanism

Usually the coping mechanism you develop to manage negative emotions from a backstory wound turns into a character flaw, something you do or believe that limits and weakens your ability to live your best creative life. Your flaw is designed to compensate for a perceived vulnerability or a sense of insecurity and feeling threatened. No matter how confident you are today, you continue to fear lessons learned from the wound inflicted in your past and remain deeply lodged in your core belief system.

Lately, you've been setting right those beliefs that had gone awry by challenging your actions and emotions and replacing them with your spiritual mantra. Then, with the storm at a breaking point, the setback that resulted in a full-blown crisis surges against the protective shield of hurt and resentment you used to cover your wound. Slammed with an onslaught of memories, original and primary emotions of fear or sorrow threaten to drown you. Your spirit gasps, having never been designed to carry so much toxicity for so long.

Whether the negative messages and view you have of yourself come from a parent, a teacher, a sibling, the collective unconscious, religious dogma, the patriarchy, or all of the above, buried emotions left to rot wreak havoc and, over time, deliver serious damage to weaken your heart and fade your spirit. Identify the impasse. And then remove it. The abyss invites you to purge the stench that holds you back.

What are the negative messages or views of yourself that hold you back?

_____

_____

_____

_____

Identifying the impasse is challenging enough. Removing it is another matter entirely. You'll likely never forget the trauma, but you can move beyond it, not by burying the memory, but by taking back all authority over your own life. Eventually, the pain doesn't hurt anymore. You move on, lighter and free.

Emotional Maturity

Now that you're forced to actually face and feel core, primary emotions, you die to who you have always been, symbolizing the death of the old to make way for the new.

Write the ancient story that creates heavy emotions in you that you're ready to release. List the negative messages to let go of based on your backstory wound. Record views you carry that limit you.

_____

_____

_____

_____

_____

_____

Next, write key words from your story above on slips of paper, find a safe spot out of the wind, and burn your words. Or write the negative messages, heavy emotions, and limiting views on ribbons and tie them to the mast of the boat. Watch as, over time, the words and past burdens fade away.

Look at this image, and evoke it by chanting as many affirmations, mantras, and pledges as needed to claw your way out of the abyss. And don't simply repeat words over and over again. For the affirmations to work, you need to believe them. Chant at night in bed and wake up feeling confident and happy.

Overlooked thoughts and emotions stuck in your mind pose a dangerous safety hazard with the potential to cause major damage. Because the abyss offers the gift of revealing those tired and obsolete burdens, incorporate them into your spiritual oath in a way that wipes them out with thoughts and emotions that bring you joy.

"I feel so free when I let go of the past and focus on letting creativity flow!"

"I've always believed things wouldn't work out for me. By sticking with my art, I see life differently and trust there's more good on the way."

"Creating without carrying the weight of my old baggage opens a well of happiness inside me."

How can the lessons emerging in the abyss become part of your pledge? Rewrite the negative thoughts and views of yourself that you're currently saying in a way that rewires your brain to meet your creative design.

_____

_____

_____

_____

_____

Lies We Tell Ourselves

A backstory wound develops when we internalize messages that belittle us, criticize us, and make us feel less than. If you were bullied as a child, likely you grow up bullying yourself. Punished for making mistakes? You grow up finding ways to punish yourself. Told you'll never be better than second best? You give up trying for first place. Criticized though you tried your best? You grow up criticizing yourself. Praised for everything you did as good? You're completely unprepared for anything less.

Early wounds in your emotional development decide how you beat yourself up for having done something wrong, not doing something right, being too slow and uncoordinated. Perhaps you rely on drugs, alcohol, cigarettes, shopping, sex, procrastination, or whatever, hoping to silence the criticism you heap on yourself. Quickly, your addiction becomes one more thing you beat yourself up about.

"I'll never amount to anything."

"I don't deserve to be happy."

"If I try, I'll only end up being a disappointment and let everyone down."

Write a lie about yourself you believe.

_____

_____

_____

_____

_____

Now reread that with the wisdom of your spirit. Rewrite this story about your past through a wise lens.

_____

_____

_____

_____

_____

_____

Draw or paint how you look and feel at your very best, in the sweet spot of the creative zone.

Chant and then write your spiritual mantra. Indicate when you last repeated it. Write if it helps when you do.

_____

_____

_____

_____

_____

THE DARK QUEEN

Before you can live in the light of your best creative life, the dark queen must be vanquished. We all have one, whether you are female or male. The only way to overpower her is to face her (your) fears, embrace her (your) pain, and fully integrate all your feelings. Only then is healing and transformation open to you.

You likely feel helpless, place your happiness in someone else's hands, wait for someone to validate you, incapacitate yourself to avoid a situation, confuse yourself when dealing with a situation or making a decision, react in anger because things don't go your way or feel fair to you, blame others for your feelings and emotions.

Many of us silence our true feelings because we are afraid to rock the boat that holds our life together. Finding your hurt and damaged self at the bottom of an abyss is a message that you've wandered off course from your truth and creative vision. All the pain in the past you can't let go of and wouldn't want to let go of drag you down. The time to finally heal, once and for all, is up to you.

Befriend your darkness. Accept the total truth about yourself. Explore your riskier emotions. Embrace your unacceptable truths. Make amends for negativity you've sent out through the misuse of your emotions.

What or who weakens you or takes your power over, or do you willingly give it up to?

_____

_____

_____

Conjure up a scene or event, conversation or misjudgment, hurt or deception. Write your feelings on the lines below.

_____

_____

_____

_____

Now, create a ritual by transferring what is most powerful onto a piece of paper. Then…burn it.

Door to the Past

Your stay in the abyss is a vulnerable time when you're dead to who you've always been. In this underworld, you're hit with all you have repressed. If you trust the Universal Story as a deep teacher, this low time, though it tortures your ego, also affords you the gift of time to deal with the past and current life-threatening moments and prepare how best to move forward.

If someone took notice of you, what would they ascertain about your backstory? Do your posture, hesitancy, boldness, physical details, dialogue, word choices, mood, tone, actions, and reactions illustrate a wound?

_____

_____

_____

_____

_____

_____

_____

Which of the above would you like to change and why?

_____

_____

_____

_____

"Getting back in the flow of my creativity helps me overcome adversity."

Untangle the emotion from your past and present relationships. Evaluate what's stacked up for you and against you. Honestly and openly face your relative strengths and weaknesses. Beneath all the different roles you play in all the different relationships—wife, mother, brother, son, aunt, guide, teacher, and mentor—lies your own individual timeless and endless spirit.

PRE-WOUNDING

Search your pre-wounding past for skills, abilities, or knowledge you lost, forgot, or had stolen. These serve you on your voyage to the end.

In your past, before you were hurt, who were you?

_____

_____

_____

_____

List your earliest strengths, fears, and joys.

_____

_____

_____

_____

Circle the ones on your list that have since changed.

Whatever happened in your past that limited your view of yourself and the world around you is not what's important. What is truly significant is the effect the wounding has had on you since. A defeatist attitude and behavior directed by narrow beliefs comes directly out of your initial wounding. The crisis burns away all that no longer serves you.

Still, you struggle. Reeling from the death of all your illusions of who you thought you were and what your place in the world was, you feel like you'll never move beyond your pain. You're tempted to give up on yourself. This is exactly when *not* to quit. You've faced death. Death leads to knowledge. You're challenged to stay with the struggle. Embrace death as well as rebirth.

Be patient and gentle with yourself. You don't suddenly live your best creative life and learn to accept and overcome doubts and negative emotions all at once. Like changing any habit, full integration takes attention, especially during stressful times when backstory wounds tend to fester and rebel.

Unprocessed wounds stunt emotional development. Wounding inflicted when you were young and hadn't yet acquired emotional maturity explains why you've been stuck in destructive patterns. Change occurs when a long succession of old patterns and habits are replaced with the new, and, with patience and courage, you experience lots of different and unfamiliar situations for the new to take hold.

Now, after all you've gone through, what reward is in it for you to persist?

_____

_____

_____

Jot your personal, inner reasons for creating a new reality.

_____

_____

_____

_____

Your answers represent gifts to prepare you for full transformation.

AN EPIPHANY

An epiphany breaks open your heart and mind. You gain new insight and "awaken" to elements of yourself you've been oblivious to or in denial about. The meaning of your epiphany does not come out of the blue. The knowledge, understanding, and new insights reflect theme elements that have been with you for your entire life.

At some point, in the new light of consciousness of all that has come before, you understand the strength and courage you've gained in your suffering and the freedom now afforded you. One of the greatest gifts you're being given is the lesson to listen to yourself and trust your inner wisdom. This new understanding is revealed in a clear way and directly affects choices and decisions you make as you move forward.

Unmask your ability to change. Clear the mists of illusion from your eyes. Find a new rhythm. No clear-cut lines mark where one phase ends and the next begins. You decide when to take action.

Let go of who you always thought yourself to be. Pull together the best parts of you. The old disappears in a puff a smoke.

TAKE ACTION

Review your Universal Story. Any action steps you didn't get to or accomplish in this phase, move to the end, phase 4—The Prize. As you rearrange sticky notes, close your eyes. Take a deep cleansing breathe. Visualize yourself performing each step. Imagine where you are, your mood, what time of day it is, and how you feel as you finish each step. Appreciate what you're learning about yourself as you journey through the abyss, as well as how you're changing.

Repacking and Crossing Over

THE UNIVERSAL STORY

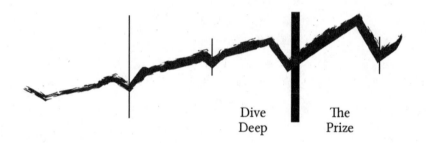

Dive
Deep

The
Prize

You've arrived at the Universal Story's third and final threshold, final for this cycle, at least. You're bruised and bedraggled and carry scars from the drama. No longer restless and impatient, you're focused and ready for the end.

> *"I accept that the road to success is littered with failure. The more failures, the closer I get."*

> *"No matter what comes, I'm finishing this!"*

> *"I kick my ego from the mix and give the piece center stage."*

True transformation comes out of a dark night. A broken heart often forces you to change. The realization that you don't like who you've become inspires you to transform. Being told your creativity is a mess ultimately strengthens you.

You may feel you have lost everything, but all the while, your spirit patiently waits for you to open your heart. Events and admonishments attempt to silence you, but as the light at the center of the universe, your spirit can never be extinguished.

You've been changed profoundly though experiencing loss. Now you're wiser and freer and ready to move out of seclusion. Personal transformation is like rebirth. Bitter winds calm. Giant waves settle. Longer days wrap you in warmth. Because of all that happened at the crisis and ensuing abyss, your energy has changed from how you used to act. Passionate about some emotions, you know which relationships to drop. You're energized to finish what you started.

It takes great courage and commitment to step into the end. On the final phase of the Universal Story for the highest good, you're well served to gather attributes, habits, and people to take forward with you.

YOU'RE NEARLY THERE

This is the time to assemble and give thanks for everything you've learned about yourself, your spirit, and life. Organize your suitcase. Toss out the attitudes, fears, beliefs, and sorrow you no longer need.

For this final ascent to The Prize, what are you leaving behind?

_____

_____

_____

_____

Now, repack your suitcase with skills and abilities and lessons learned about endurance, perseverance, boundaries, acceptance, your strengths, and the wisdom that now defines you.

What lessons have you learned about yourself and your craft that you plan to take with you on the final ascent to The Prize?

_____

_____

_____

_____

What gifts have you learned about yourself that you didn't know, haven't been using, or didn't appreciate as strengths?

_____

_____

_____

_____

_____

The more "all in" you are as you cross over to the end, the better. The challenges are no easier; in fact, they rise quickly in intensity, but now you face them willingly and fearlessly as you complete your outer creativity goal.

You faced your backstory wound. Think back further. Recall the days when you possessed childlike wonder, ran and jumped, sang to yourself, ate dirt and climbed trees, twirled, broke things, threw things, and giggled uncontrollably. Free of painful stories, you're lighter now. As a result, your spiritual goal may be vastly different. Your deepest beliefs about yourself no longer fight against the spiritual qualities you embrace. With the past healed or on its way to being healed, you lean in to your best self.

Write the spiritual mantra you take with you as you go forward. Tuck a copy of what you write in your pocket, your car; tape it to the refrigerator.

_____

_____

_____

Get Moving

While still grappling with the implosion you recently suffered, you spot an underwater tunnel. A light glows in the distance, beckoning you forward. For the first time in days, months, or years, you feel hopeful. Ready to finish your creative goal, suddenly you have a sense of the eleventh hour. You question what you are waiting for. Granted a moment of clarity, you take control of your reality and get moving. You're ready to finish your creativity goal and celebrate your spiritual goal. You're ready to move from isolation to reconnection.

Do you have enough motivation and energy to keep going to the end?   *Yes*   *No*

Are you still fulfilling steps toward your creativity project?   *Yes*   *No*

If no, what's missing to activate you again?

_____

_____

_____

_____

_____

How many more steps until you reach the end?

_____

_____

_____

Are you on track to meet your deadline?   *Yes*   *No*

If no, what will help?

   Change deadline   *Show up for your art more frequently*   *Focus*   *Other*

If you circled "other," explain here.

_____

_____

_____

_____

_____

THRESHOLD GUARDIANS

Remember the threshold guardians from your first two crossings? Well, they're back, and they've brought their friends. Killer whales pick at dark emotions from adversaries. A stingray, a great white shark, and a blue-ringed octopus block the tunnel entrance and next phase of the Universal Story. Dark forces in society, in other people, and in technology, religion, customs, government, and secret societies are intent—consciously or unconsciously—on luring you away from change and continually test your resolve. Ready to advance, your flaws become strengths. The gatekeepers cringe at your light and swim away. A backstory wound resolves itself.

You're presented with two questions.

- Do you stay where you are?

- Do you move forward?

Your decision defines your future. How you react now prepares the ground for tomorrow and the next time you're faced with a difficulty, hit a wall, or feel a failure. The emotions you project as you're creating directly relate to how you're feeling in this moment. Don't change how you feel or fix your feelings. Now that you're awake, accept that this moment is happening as a gift to experience more of the unknown.

You've learned lessons that your flaws determined. You're stronger having accepted and embraced your imperfections. Each learning-growth-change-transformation cycle plays out in ways that uniquely match your specific spiritual needs.

What emotions do you take forward?

_____

_____

_____

_____

_____

You've gained a higher consciousness capable of seeing all sides of yourself, your creativity project, and your goal. The fear you'll fail again, as in past setbacks and wrong turns, no longer squeezes you like a vise.

In charge of your life, dreams emerge. Connected to your spirit, you're ready to give voice to what you and only you can convey.

A THRESHOLD

This final threshold is a symbol, as all entrances are, that awaits a decision. From crisis through the abyss, some creatives arrive at this spot quickly. Others take a long time.

"Burnout lasted six months last year."

Hit with a series of spirit-crushing black moments not so long ago, I took five years to fully separate from the intervening abyss. Ostracized and humiliated, my sluggishness came partly from having no idea how to get out. The landscape leached familiar themes of betrayal and deception, unspoken since childhood. Even lost in the darkest hours of my life, my business thrived. That's because the only time I seemed able to stop crying was when I was working. Holding on by a thread, I grappled with how to heal. I beat myself up. Retreated. Threw blame on others. Seethed. Grieved. Shut down.

What's important is what happens after you crawl through the tunnel and then stand up. Brush yourself off. Walk away from the abyss. What's coming is unknown. You're okay with not knowing.

You face two choices.

- Resist what is, and surrender to being a victim.

- Yield to what is, and become a victor.

Circle the one you will choose to pursue.

Most thresholds are invisible, meaning you don't know when you've crossed over. Other entries are significant enough to be called "portals" or "grand entrances" to new and exotic worlds. Your old life was known, often joyous and sometimes miserable. Passing through the eye of a needle, falling down a rabbit hole, crossing a bridge, venturing into a forest, and traveling through space are scary and unknown. One side is intent. The other involves action.

What does the threshold you're standing at look like? Do you sense what is on the other side? If so, describe what's waiting for you. If not, describe how the mystery feels.

_____

_____

_____

_____

_____

The next phase of the voyage stands open, inviting discovery. Something *has* happened. Something else *will* happen. Only this exact moment, as you stand before the threshold, is real. When you're most convinced you cannot go forward is precisely the moment to forge ahead. You've lost your confidence. It's time to reclaim it. The depth of your fear and resistance determines the potential for profound change. Take with you the promise of something new.

"I keep coming back to my work because it's intrinsic to my being."

TAKE ACTION

As you move forward, follow your heart. What you wish for or need in each moment miraculously appears to confirm your new beliefs. Someone materializes, seemingly out of nowhere, offers small or significant help, and then disappears as randomly as they first appeared. A grisly old artist with no teeth told me about a famous potter who once had been kind to him and how aides like that were now and forevermore known as Potter People. When you most need help, they're everywhere. Keep an eye out for them.

Has it ever happened to you that when you needed help, suddenly someone appeared with the required aid, never to be seen or heard from again?

Yes   *No*

What did the help and experience mean to you?

With a backstory wound, we reject the sweetness of life and are made to feel ruined, undeserving, tarnished, damaged, less than. Wounds stunt our emotional growth and shrink our capacity to receive our good and abundance in the universe. That doesn't mean we consciously turn away the good and abundance. It means we only embrace what we believe we deserve, which is a small fraction of the great wealth available to us. All the rest spills into the ocean.

Every day, outstretch your arms and embrace your good. Daily, stretch a bit farther. Embrace a bit more.

Clean and tidy and organize your notes, your studio, and workspace. Celebrate the fresh air.

Across the threshold, I offer my hand.

In your own time… Let's finish this.

PHASE 4

The Prize

The
Prize

Ambushed by hurricane winds and king waves hell-bent on crushing you, you survived the lowest point in your odyssey. Emerging from the darkness, you reenter the land of the present-day living. You're a changed person, ready to practice new beliefs, master your craft, and redirect your energies toward finishing what you started. Except this time, light energy pulses at a level higher than when you started.

Angst and hard times, worry and fear don't just vanish because you're now on your way to your triumph. In every moment, you're given the choice of what you wish to believe and how you wish to behave. Before your dark night, you rolled your eyes at others' wacky ideas. Now that others roll their eyes at your work, you're aware of how dismissive that simple act is. You were judged harshly and are now more sensitive to how you judge others. Or you dared to pursue a creative vision, it didn't work out how you thought it would, and you're ready to puzzle a new way forward. These changes don't happen effortlessly. The prize at the end comes after an intense rise in energy, as seen in the Universal Story. That same energy flutters through your body with expectancy.

As you enter the fourth and final phase of the Universal Story, step away from the details of living your best creative life and view the entire panorama of your life. Notice where you made choices and how those choices affect your creativity and form the beliefs you live by. Though life often feels random, you know better now. The cause and effect of your choices compels you to accept responsibility for your life.

List major choices you've made and how those choices affect how you live now.

_____

_____

_____

_____

List the major choices you've made with your creativity project and how you anticipate those choices affecting the outcome.

_____

_____

_____

_____

_____

Take a further step back from your Universal Story. Blur your eyes and look again. The ups and downs you've been through merge into moments when you became wiser and more forgiving and creative. Even the most difficult challenges add beauty to one giant mosaic. You choose which pieces go into creating your design. The pattern reads your future.

"I gained a sense of authenticity. Now when I write and speak, I'm being myself, sharing who I am and how I perceive the world around me."

"The two greatest gifts I've received from living a creative life are cellular level satisfaction and gratification."

"I'm tougher now and don't take things so personally."

How have you changed since starting your creativity and spiritual goals?

_____

_____

_____

_____

_____

_____

Forgiveness and Gratitude

The healing that started in the abyss continues through the mastery of two life skills—forgiveness and gratitude. Forgive and be forgiven. As you go about finishing your creativity goal, give thanks for all you've learned and acquired through the tests and trials you've encountered. Tell yourself whatever you need to get yourself moving.

"Do the next step to completion. Keep it small."

"I'm me, learning as I go."

"With this new feeling, I can learn anything and attempt anything without thinking it has to be perfect."

"I'm learning to actually enjoy the challenges."

What do you tell yourself to keep going?

_____

_____

_____

What happens next is determined in large part by the quality of your heart. You may not be able to articulate the purpose of your life, but you know now without words that you are the treasure. You forgive yourself for choices in the past. You're grateful for your emotions as helpful messengers and…are no longer ruled by them.

FORGIVENESS

Forgiveness embraces understanding as an act of grace. The more compassion you practice toward yourself, and the more you let go of others' transgressions, the more you find to forgive. Like those fears you carry around with you that you're unlovable. Or the sadness that pulls at you that you're unworthy of being loved and living a creative life. As feelings of loneliness wash over you without overtaking you, let them go. Forgive each bit of sadness and fear, sorrow and worry you've allowed in.

More and more, you catch yourself early, before you're completely submerged in thoughts and feelings that drown your creative energy. You acknowledge and explore how you're feeling. Then you chant grateful thoughts and feelings. Consciously choosing to think and feel differently is a form of forgiveness.

Holding on weighs you down. Thinking differently sets you free. Grudges trip you up. Your thoughts and feelings create your outlook.

How do you rate your ability to forgive other people?

Nonexistent	*Poor*	*Good*	*Excellent*	*Easy*

How easily do you forgive yourself?

Nonexistent	*Poor*	*Good*	*Excellent*	*Easy*

Below, list everyone you believe should forgive you and apologize to you on one side. On the other side, include anyone you believe you should apologize to and forgive. Be sure to include yourself in both lists.

_____   _____

_____   _____

_____   _____

_____   _____

_____   _____

Forgive Yourself

At first, the lifetime of damage you've inflicted on yourself wins against your longing to sink into the creative womb. The longer you practice your spiritual mantra, the stronger you become. Patient and kind, you name your muse and wait in your creative space. Lack of self-worth pokes out from unexplored regions of your heart.

Slowly, you understand how one purposeful and strong dimension of your motivation to live your best creative life stands in direct conflict with another strong dimension of your motivation—to protect yourself at all cost.

Any bitterness, self-pity, blaming, or shaming you carry represents hot spots left to heal. Every time you're genuinely happy and hopeful and creative, a deeply embedded belief lies dormant, waiting to flare up about your zero personal worth. Mourn and forgive angry and resentful feelings and whatever else you uncover with your light.

In many ways, the most difficult part of moving forward is learning how to forgive. And to forgive others means first you have to forgive yourself.

"I forgive myself for holding on for so long."

"I forgive myself for the judgments I made about my life and the lives of others."

"I forgive and release all limitations I believe about myself."

List what you forgive yourself for—for not being perfect, for disappointing others and yourself, for failing, for not trying, for not believing, for giving up, for…

_____

_____

_____

_____

_____

_____

Forgive Others

With thoughts of personal release, I sat at my desk to write a talk about forgiveness for a video series I was shooting. As I explored what it means to forgive, I suddenly found myself in a sinkhole. The more excuses I came up with about why one person or some painful event didn't deserve to be forgiven, the deeper I sank. I don't remember what I said about forgiveness on camera. I do know that getting to a place of forgiveness took me another two stubborn years.

To truly forgive means completely letting go. I could have saved myself a lot of time if I hadn't resisted that idea for so long. Let go of the hurt? I couldn't figure out how. Let the wrongdoers off the hook? I refused to accept the injustice. Let me off the hook? Instead, I tucked away the pain as insurance against it happening again.

Then, on a day like any other day, I found holding on to negativity exhausting and a ridiculous expenditure of energy. What was I doing leaving festering wounds to worsen and spread and even become deadly when I could heal and move on?

At the time, I was purging a casita of everything old that no longer delighted me. A bunch of grudges I'd lugged around landed in the loads I donated to a local charity. A stack of complaints and judgments ended up at the recycling center. Immediately, the energy around me lightened.

Letting go of the past clears room for three things to focus on to the triumphant end:

- Achieve your external creativity goal.

- Choose to be happy.

- Create in meaningful ways.

Letting go lightens your energy as you rise to peak action, doing something you could not have done at the beginning of the odyssey. You needed to experience every bump along the way to contribute to your ultimate transformation.

GRATITUDE

Gratitude is a great place to begin your quest of forgiveness. The radical inner change you've experienced may have come as a close call, closer than you dare admit aloud, but you survived. Give thanks for being alive. Everyone gets this, but not everyone seizes the chance to pursue art purely for the love of creating something out of nothing but a whim.

As you practice gratitude, give thanks to the people in your life who irritate, frustrate, and anger you, who make you retreat and give up, or who turn you jealous and defensive. Thank them for the countless opportunities to practice not getting hooked into the drama of an argument, an insult, an old unproductive behavior. The more practice you get, the more practice you find you need to access patience and acceptance while attempting to be nonreactive and nonjudgmental.

Who is the person or persons who bring out the worst in you?

_____

_____

_____

_____

Eventually, you give thanks for everything that's happened, because both the good and the bad made you who you are today.

Creativity opens your brain and enhances all your senses. Colors turn brighter.

"I replace my fear with blind trust that I am supported and all is well."

"Doing something creative in my life makes me feel balanced and fulfilled."

"Living a creative life is not without pitfalls or setbacks, but I get to be more truly who I am than I otherwise would."

As someone who makes things, over the years, you've gained many gifts and lessons and insights.

Give thanks for all you've learned. Thank you for…

_____

_____

_____

_____

_____

_____

CONSCIOUS CHANGE

You're in the process of conscious change. Those around you may not like you expressing yourself. They have their own patterns, one of which is to keep you in the same category they've always kept you.

Be sensitive to people and situations that challenge you. You are not looking to change anyone else. You're not looking to get into a power struggle, break anyone's spirit, or create drama. Identify emotional reactions that reflect fear and unhappiness, evaluate why, and then visualize true and positive behavior. As you gain stability and mastery of your emotions, you're learning to be who you are, not who someone else decided you should be.

Practice a daily act of loving kindness to those who love and support you. Write down what you do, to whom, and how your act of gratitude feels.

_____

_____

_____

_____

_____

_____

_____

Imagine an act of loving kindness to those you feel are difficult, against you, and a challenge. Write down what you do, to whom, and how it makes you feel.

_____

_____

_____

_____

_____

_____

_____

Creative energy continually reshapes your life, reveals the meaning behind why things happen, and offers mysterious support that aligns with your goals and intentions. Go after the juicier, riskier, high-reward inspirations and opportunities. Shake things up. A creative idea radiates a force that attracts what it needs to expand and develop. You feel the pull. Explore.

Failure

You know you're healed when you find yourself giving thanks even for your failures. Failures, more than anything else, direct your life course. Rejection letters, rude treatment, disrespect, snubs, poor critiques, negative reviews—worse than the painful moments themselves are your reactions to them. Now that you know that, you sit with your disappointment, humiliation, and the urge to fight or run. Rather than resort to an old addiction that only makes you feel more like a loser, you forgive yourself. Then you trust that this too imparts a helpful message, lesson, new skill, understanding, and ultimate acceptance. And so you stay open and encourage yourself.

Failure is good. It's where learning begins. Well, that is, so long as you don't shut down. If you identified your emotional set point as fear or sorrow, be hyper-careful not to succumb to self-blame and victimhood.

The severity of the crisis you experience in phase 3 and how long you spend in the abyss can actually shift your emotional set point. Often, people in the depths of despair cower in fear that something else bad is about to happen. Or they shelter themselves in sorrow. If they are fortunate, ancient memories of a happier time begin to surface. A conscious decision is all that's needed to begin adjusting your set point to happiness.

"I choose to be happy."

"I embrace happiness."

"Joy, joy, joy!"

The Decision Is Yours

Failure implies the challenge is over. Nothing is truly over until you decide it is. An acceptance of failure releases troubling, incomplete, toxic, sad, and scary stories you made up over the years about yourself and about life in general. With the illusionary stories, you release emotions you've unconsciously adopted as your own. You reevaluate the cultural and institutional beliefs you were raised with to determine your own personal and true beliefs of what is good and evil, true and false. Having fallen, you redefine, restore, reinstate, return, and renew all that is dear.

FOCUS ON FINISHING

You have changed. You see the world differently, and your place in the world has altered. Every action you take, every rule you break, every risk and every challenge you meet signify transformation has begun.

Don't expect anyone else to notice your changes as everyone and everything carries on as usual. Gatekeepers loiter around thresholds. You feel their eyes on you. Take any action now that betrays your true nature or utter a single word of doubt about whether you're ready for the end…anticipate an ambush.

When you turn away from the drama and focus on finishing, everything—except the step you're on right now—drops away. You integrate more of you into your work. Lost in creating, suddenly you feel illuminated from within. Your hands turn translucent.

Emotional circuits that push you to apologize and rationalize, explain and complain, and that grip and block and trap you are undergoing a dynamic change. As you gather the courage and patience to fully experience what you're honestly feeling—without thought or judgment, but purely at a sensory and physiological level, old circuits weaken. New circuits activate change through the continual use of your spiritual pledge.

A peaceful connection to your creativity is the key to grace. Rewrite your creativity goal to include your deadline. Define "finishing." Be specific about what comes next with the work—the writing, painting, jewelry, and the music you finish.

_____

_____

_____

_____

_____

What is your purpose for completing your creativity goal?

_____

_____

_____

_____

_____

If you intend to share your work beyond your studio and notebook, camera and workshop, jot those steps on sticky notes and affix to the end of the Universal Story.

_____

_____

_____

_____

_____

The rewards for staying true to your vow and finishing your creativity goal are many. Write a description of the prize waiting for you at the end of this odyssey.

_____

_____

_____

_____

_____

_____

When awarded your prize, how will that moment feel and what will it look like? What will you be doing? Draw a picture or write about the experience of bringing a creative idea to life and following through to the end.

_____

_____

_____

_____

_____

_____

TAKE ACTION

If you initially set one month as your deadline, you have ten days left to complete your outer creativity goal. One step per day translates into ten steps to reach your goal. No easier than the middle of your odyssey, reaching the end is much more difficult. The major difference now is you've gained important information about yourself, your patterns and habits, your beliefs, and your creativity. This is a great time to firm up exactly what you intend to accomplish.

Break your creativity goal into two parts.

- State your goal of finishing what you started by a specific deadline.

- Include what you intend to do with what you create.

Record that goal here.

_____

_____

_____

Tribe of Supporters

A sense of urgency builds as the deadline for your creativity goal approaches. With your creative life ablaze, you find yourself using all the lessons and wisdom gained to finish. In a rush to reach your triumph, you snap the next sticky note from above the line of your Universal Story. A step closer to completion, with just a few steps left.

At the end of this cycle, another goal awaits to send you on yet another voyage toward change and transformation. Your triumph, on the other hand, stays with you—a new skill you've mastered, insight into what is on the other side of the veil you keep hidden away, a newfound confidence, and the decision to be happy.

How has your life changed now that you're nearly finished? How does life look around you?

_____

_____

_____

_____

_____

If this will be your debut, the first portrait you've painted, the only vase you've thrown—the first artistic goal you've ever achieved—celebrate! Savor this moment. Life will never be the same. As fabulous as the next time around will be, like your first love, nothing will ever quite compare in intensity and passion to the first one you created with open-hearted abandon and pure joy.

TESTS CONTINUE

As you bring your ideas to fruition, your core beliefs continue to be tested ten thousand times. Don't believe you deserve to live your best creative life? You won't. You believe you deserve creative time to yourself? Only you can make that happen.

Celebrate your attempts to assert yourself. So long passive, you're often challenged to find that delicate balance between strident bullying and wishy-washy vagueness.

Which of the following is true for you?

- You are used to speaking up for yourself.

- Being vocal about your creativity is a new skill you're learning.

When you do speak up for yourself, you find that the problem, issue, or conflict isn't all that important—whereas if you'd remained silent, words would have gnawed at you for minutes, hours, days...

You've likely also found that speaking, writing, painting your truth means you first have to know your truth. Often that comes out of trial and error—working toward standing your ground as a reflection of a true inner belief. As you hear your words being spoken, revise what feels false and then try again until you find yourself freely expressive. Being genuine shows courage and trust and is spiritually significant.

For you to celebrate and, indeed, complete these last few steps of your creativity goal, the ability to speak up and be heard is a gift.

MEETING NEW PEOPLE

As you continue to forgive yourself, family, and old friends, you begin meeting new people. You're different now, so the people you're drawn to change.

Every medium creates its own world. The longer you delve into writing scripts for feature films, taking classes, and attending conferences, the more you find a few key figures dominate and how small the screenwriting world really is. Someone you meet at a workshop invites you to a critique group she's putting together. A friend you've slowly come to appreciate tells you about an upcoming grant to support a current work of art. Your local bookstore announces a work-in-progress reading. You spot a performance art class forming in your neighborhood.

Supporters

As you meet new people, consider forming a tribe of like-minded creatives. No one knows better the rush of excitement than another creative.

One way to form a tribe is to throw a party or initiate a ritual. As practice in reaching out to others, invite people to commemorate your and their achievements. Ask people you've met in the creative arts, people who inspire, challenge, support, and believe in you. After the party, come together from time to time to discuss your progress and setbacks, listen, awaken, support, and inspire one another. Tribe members listen as you express your intentions. No one attempts to fix anything. They simply serve as silent witnesses to your process. As you continue together in your artistic careers, the group may begin critiquing each other's work and intentions with suggestions, feedback, and support. Perform rituals to highlight major energetic and creative milestones.

Communicating your truths moves emotions from your body out into the light. Serving as a witness for others allows you a broader understanding of your fears and breakthroughs, hurt and transformation. Your supporters hold you accountable as you complete short-term steps. Together, you share your hopes and fears, struggles and stories. In solidarity, you remind each other what you're doing and why and are comforted by the universality of the creative process.

Do you benefit from being accountable to someone else to keep you on track?

Yes   *No*

List anyone your currently know or anything that has the potential to support you in achieving your goal.

_____

_____

_____

_____

_____

List anyone or anything that grows your energy, inspires you, and encourages you.

_____

_____

_____

_____

_____

Eventually, you surrender. You trust your inner guidance. Creative energy flows unobstructed into spiritual wisdom and wholeness. You draw strength from your work. No one knows all the nuances of your art but you. Therefore, the best-case scenario is when the greatest supporter of your work is you. Sadly, this is not always the case. If your tribe consists of you, your spirit, your creativity, and no one else, be sure you've made friends with yourself, because you're on your own during all the ups and downs. Until you're completely rid of your propensity for being negative with yourself, find someone you trust to check in with you from time to time for encouragement.

For you who are more extroverted, creating a tribe of supporters and compatible creatives who radiate out from your inner core is a welcome relief.

Your Best

As you attempt to be your best, if you run into anyone who sees you that way, band together. Of the creatives you see at a book reading or an open-studio event, you're energetically drawn toward certain people. Your intuition keeps nudging you to strike up a conversation. Risk reaching out. Foster relationships with those who treat you with respect and leave you energized and hopeful. As one person's patience and generosity and kindness inspires you, return the good fortune by showering others with kindheartedness.

Become aware of the nonverbal emotional cues you give out that can support or hinder what you want, especially if the person or group you're communicating with is savvy enough to discern whether what you're *saying* you believe and feel is actually true. Often those you would most like to sway in your favor easily interpret what your eye movements, lack of eye contact, interruptions, shoulder shrugs, mouth gestures, and other facial expressions are really saying.

Do you nod and smile when listening to others, or frown and squint, or look away, distracted by your phone? Generally, how do you respond when listening to others?

SHARING YOUR WORK WITH OTHERS

When you first decided on your creativity goal, you may have included steps to take once you have finished your piece. Post artwork, jewelry, or lotions and creams on Instagram. Set up an Etsy account and sell your work. Enter an art show. Eventually, all creatives are faced with the dilemma of what to do with what they create. My mother knitted sweaters and socks and blankets for all of us and for worthy causes, painted pictures over pictures on canvas, needlepointed and wove textiles for presents. If you're friends with a creative baker or artist or card maker, you likely receive lovely handcrafted gifts.

Finishing what you start is a ritual that completes the cycle—birth, growth, change, and transformation. For some, finishing is when you share the magnificence and power of your work with the world. Your goal is met when you help find a safe harbor for what you create.

"I require a destination at the end of the creative journey and that destination for me is readers. If I get one reader who loves my characters as much as I do, that is success."

"Each time I post a photo or painting on social media feels like crossing the finish line."

"Sharing my art, connecting, and teaching."

All of these are honorable ways of finishing by bringing your work into the light—a reading, a performance, a show, a contest, a critique group. They all have a place in living your best creative life.

As the final part of your external creativity goal, did you challenge yourself to show your work to others?

Yes   No

If yes, in what ways do you intend to share your creativity?

_____

_____

_____

_____

If no, is sharing your work something you aspire to in the future?

On Display

You begin the steps toward putting your work on display, and immediately, as the outside world gets involved, things get complicated. Your quiet oasis fills with voices and feedback. Creative purity gets buried under critiques, opinions, attitudes, comments, and judgments. Surrounded by outside influences, you can barely conjure up your original vision. Before you know it, you're juggling more even as you've been purging for less.

The steps you take to share your work with others expose what you resist and offer opportunities to learn how to work around interference. Don't expect to get this right immediately. Learning how to interact with others with grace often takes a lifetime to achieve, and even then, we're still learning.

Your inner life has changed to make room for your creativity. Now your outer life takes a more active part in your creative life. And these parts you'll either love or avoid.

IN SERVICE TO YOUR ART

Is a creative project ever really done? Countless writers still find words to change in their published works. Artists squint at their art hanging on gallery walls and speak of adding shading here or a splash of light there. Yes, your deadline signifies you've reached the end of the program. Your piece, on the other hand, may take years to complete. That's why, when crafting an outer creativity goal, you were asked to include a form of outreach to signify the completion of this current step in the overall project.

Living a creative life is not only about creating. It's also about being in service to your creativity. If you showed your work before you or it was ready and a very dark night blew up in your face, you're likely to be apprehensive about showing it again.

The steps you take to share your work with others deepen what you're learning about your emotional reactions to praise and criticism. At first you grapple with how to balance your time between pursuing creativity and sharing your work with others. Many successful artists resent the time stolen from creating their art to promote finished works. They are two different skill sets, and both are important, especially so because what you bring new to the table may move others around their blind spots.

Of the steps left on the Universal Story, how many involve outreach?

_____

How do you feel about sharing your work?

_____

_____

_____

_____

_____

_____

What are you looking for from sharing your work? Write a set of guidelines.

_____

_____

_____

_____

_____

_____

_____

_____

_____

_____

How will you feel when you receive negative feedback about your creativity project?

_____

_____

_____

_____

_____

_____

How will you feel when you receive positive feedback about your creativity project?

_____

_____

_____

_____

_____

_____

How will positive or negative feedback affect your creative productivity?

_____

_____

_____

_____

_____

_____

Sharing your work with others is an invitation for people to express their opinions. First, be sure you're ready. Often creatives are afraid to believe fully in their talent so they turn to others to confirm or deny their creative worth. When you ask, don't surrender your power by thinking that someone else knows more than you. Fall into that trap and you begin changing your work to please others, and you'll end up not pleasing anyone. Be respectful of what others say. Then, heed your own counsel.

Darkness Returns

As you approach your deadline, the wind gusts. An early spring storm hits. Rain falls. Waves grow steep, rocking the boat. As you turn seasick, you become painfully aware of how often you still have to practice moving out of dark emotional moods and reactions and replacing them with light and more manageable and productive feelings. Rather than peaceful and calm, you often find yourself agitated and anxious. Rather than trusting you'll succeed, you grow resentful and suspicious. Defensive and often feeling defeated, you struggle to find your confidence.

The longer and further you travel into the Universal Story, the better able you are to sense what's happening and why, as well as what comes next—energetically anyway. Repeat your spiritual pledge. Rather than continue to stamp old stuck patterns into your biology and ruin your health, forge new emotional pathways in a more productive direction.

TABLES TURN

In step 11, you identified whether you lean more toward being an introvert or an extrovert. While caught up in the steps creating your art, an inclination to thrive in quiet and solitude serves you well. If, on the other hand, your skin crawls when you're holed up alone, you struggle. Now, the tables turn. Introverts often find painful the steps in sharing their work with others, while extroverts shine in the public eye.

Either way, these next steps thrust you into an exotic sea filled with new rules and expectations. Something is bound to uncover a hidden hurt filled with darkness and gloom. Be prepared. Have a strategy to appreciate and explore your feelings.

If you don't have anyone you can ask for reminders of your magnificence, remind yourself that you no longer believe being flawed is bad and not good enough. Being flawed is the human condition.

As you're feeling strong and hopeful, write down what you long to hear when you're most lost.

_____

_____

_____

_____

You find yourself spending less and then no time nurturing relationships that don't matter. Instead, you spend the time you have creating and nurturing friends who nurture you, sharing wisdom and support. You find you cannot always please everyone while also pleasing yourself. You'll never win over everyone. That's why those people you do win over are precious.

List anyone and everyone who nurtures you, as well as how they encourage you.

_____

_____

_____

_____

_____

_____

TAKE ACTION

You repeat your spiritual oath so many times, it begins to lose its meaning and power because you no longer consciously hear and take in the affirmation. In the same way, after repeatedly seeing the notes you left reminding you to repeat your oath, you no longer consciously see them anymore. They lose their meaning.

If the oath you chant now is working, simply move the reminders to unexpected places. When you see them, you'll be surprised into remembering.

If, however, it's time to renew your oath, do so now.

_____

_____

_____

Chant your oath everywhere you go. When you can, chant aloud. Around others, chant to yourself. The more locations where you practice and the more circumstances and people you chant around, the more generalized your association with your message of love.

STEP 18

Outer Fulfillment

THE UNIVERSAL STORY

You did it! You successfully met your deadline. Sure, it may have required extreme fortitude and sheer determination for you to arrive here on time. All the energy for the past month has been traveling to the final and most intense energy marker in the entire Universal Story—the Triumph.

Do you feel triumphant about reaching your deadline?   *Yes*   *No*

If you circled yes, how are you celebrating your achievement?

_____

_____

_____

_____

_____

If you circled no, explain.

_____

_____

_____

Do you feel triumphant about your creative piece?   *Yes*   *No*

If you circled yes, describe what you like best.

_____

_____

_____

_____

_____

If you circled no, explain.

_____

_____

_____

Did you complete your external creativity goal? Circle your answer.   *Yes*   *No*

If no, what's left to accomplish?

_____

_____

_____

From the Universal Story's highest peak, you have a 360-degree view of your life as one droplet in a vast Sea of Creativity. The crowning glory of living a creative life comes each time you manifest your dream by finishing all the way to the end. And you did just that. You succeeded at reaching the deadline for your creativity goal. Every sticky note with every step led you to outer success and inner fulfillment.

"I consider myself creatively successful because I'm working. So long as I continue to develop my practice and hone my craft, I'm successful."

"Timing is everything. I trust more in the process and in the timing now, and so I feel successful whenever a project comes to completion."

"I feel like a success when I finish a project I'm genuinely proud of."

TRIUMPH

The energy pulsating at the Triumph is represented in as many different forms as there are people—the achievement of a vision, an accomplishment, a victory, a satisfaction, a feat, a joy.

Circle your definition of success:

    Prosperity   *Fame*   *Respect*   *Peace of Mind*   *Other*

If you circled "other," explain.

_____

_____

_____

_____

"I no longer resent the feedback from my critique group. I appreciate that good work is not perfect. Both the process and the product have lovely and inevitable flaws."

"I rejoice when I complete a chapter or plunge into researching a new book."

"Writing is a complete joy. It doesn't all have to be profound. It doesn't have to become a 'bestseller.' It doesn't even have to culminate in a finished book. Success is simply being proud of what I've accomplished."

You suddenly grasp something striking in its simplicity. Merely reaching your deadline is enough. Once there, you find you're not wildly excited about what you created and not much interested in sharing the outcome with others. It's not unusual for a creative to go through a thousand deaths to find that the 1001st beginning holds your prize.

Or you're quite satisfied with what you've created. Your piece may not be fully finished, but you stuck with your goal all the way to your deadline. That's success. Where you end up—how near or how far from completion—isn't as important as meeting the deadline you set early on for your creativity goal.

ONE FINAL CEREMONY

You've moved beyond the everyday physical reality to a place of mystical dimensions that transcends form and time and space—your spirit. As a result, you've learned to listen to the stirrings of you inner life and gained spiritual wisdom. This rite of passage into living your best creative life has landed you in an entirely new reality or returned you to your old world as a changed person. Before you disembark, you have one final ceremony to perform.

The gatekeepers to the mystical realm of creativity grant you entry into a special group of creators. This time, you cross from being who you were to someone who creates things. To complete your initiation, you're granted a new title: artist, writer, potter, musician, designer…

What title do you give yourself now that you've completed your creativity goal?

_____

_____

If at first the title feels false or you feel like a fraud or unworthy, remember, whether famous or beginner, all creatives do the exact same thing—show up for their art. So long as you continue to create, wear with pride the title fitting of you as a maker of things!

THE NEXT STEP

As you usher your work out into the world, tag along as a chaperone to ensure your art is well received. Promote yourself. Get beta-readers, a critique group, interviews, reviews, and blurbs. Take classes. Hone your skills. Keep practicing.

As you do, appreciate that as helpful as feedback is about what's not working, just as, or more so, is learning what others perceive as your strengths, what you're good at. Coming from your strength to address your weakness is spiritually energizing. Thus, when critiqued, always ask first for what is working before learning what isn't.

Even as you get tangled up with outreach, remember, living a creative life is about creating. In every moment, bring your special flair. Imagining something new, inventive, helpful, beautiful, meaningful, and lovely is only the beginning. Enacting all the steps necessary to manifest the vision and reach the end is what truly counts. Never stop. And don't get stuck on the first things you complete. Keep practicing. Keep challenging yourself. Keep trying new ways to express yourself.

The true meaning of success is joyfully creating every day.

REJECTION

When you put your work on display, you invite in helpful people. You also risk rejection. Staying optimistic and inspired while dealing with rejection is never easy. When what's being rejected comes from such a pure place of surrender inside of you, a refusal, rebuff, criticism, panning, or ridicule hurts like hell.

> "After being unable to write a thing for several years due to a harsh and biased critique, finally I was emotionally able to ask her about her response to my work. She admitted she read my work at a very difficult time in her life and was envious of my journey. Thus her harsh response. After our discussion, I was able to move on to another project. I've yet to be able to pull that particular project back on the work table, but I'm slowly getting there, after many years. I'm very careful now about who reads and responds to my work. A negative group or an envious writing partner can be devastating to a writer."

For some, when confronted with rejection, you meet your old self again. Before you give your power away, tear yourself down, and moan about why you ever thought you could do this, learn to appreciate yourself for you. Your value and the value of your spirit are far more magnificent than reviews or the number of followers you have.

As you begin fully living a creative life by both creating and sharing, focus on staying in balance. Do not give up the internal habit of creating every day as you develop an external habit of reaching out, publicizing, teaching, and sending work off to contests, agents, and shows. Keep your momentum for your creativity moving in a positive direction. Don't get so caught up in promoting the project you just finished that you become a one-book-wonder and stop creating.

When you stay true to the creative muse, you ignore others' dictates about what you should think and what you could do. You no longer try to numb your pain or be someone you're not or believe something outside of yourself will make you whole.

Self-Care

As the demands on you and your creativity and spirit increase, self-care becomes essential. When I started writing, I fell in love with transcending the real world to where my energy was light and my spirit alive. Tucked in creativity, no longer subjected to emotions and limitations, I wrote obsessively. I'd get hungry, and still, I wrote. I'd get tired and kept writing anyway. I paid for my wonted ways by getting stiff or sick, or hurting myself and sleeping for days until I eventually learned the benefits of exercise and movement, healthy eating, and a good night's sleep to creativity.

Food. If you're prone to eating junk food while you're in the zone of creativity, consider shopping before you begin. Stock your refrigerator with organic, real food that grows out of the ground. Prepare meals ahead of time so it's easy to fill your body with nourishing food. Keep hydrated. Drink water.

What is your relationship with food?

_____

_____

_____

_____

_____

Sleep. Earlier in the program, I discussed the value in seeding your dreams with requests for answers or inspiration and then remembering to write down what comes to you as you awaken. Sleep is the time your body heals and restores and reenergizes itself.

How well do you sleep at night?

Poorly   *Intermittently*   *Good*   *Deep and rested*

Exercise. Though religious traditions recommend focusing on things that are above and not on things that are of the earth, such a practice isolates you from Mother Nature. Your energy grows light in nature and your spirit thrives. Take breaks from creating to move in the natural world. Learn to watch for signs. Listen to the messages in the tides. Gain wisdom from the earth. Reclaim a sense of wonder.

How often do you wander in nature and let your spirit play?

Daily   *Weekly*   *Never*

List three things you've done today that demonstrate that you have your best interests at heart.

_____

_____

_____

TAKE ACTION

The creativity goal you've been working on may have more steps to complete. Or the work you've been doing inspires another creativity idea, something entirely different.

> *"I want to switch media to learn a whole new skill set. My storytelling and interviewing talents serve this new medium well."*

> *"I plan to start a project that scares me but is also more meaningful to me."*

> *"Create steel art—welding, torching, plasma cutting, hammering, grinding—you name it. I want to try it."*

Whether what comes next is new or an extension of what you've been focused on, take time to revel in what you've accomplished.

STEP 19

Inner Fulfillment

Along the way to the deadline for your creativity goal, you became hypervigilant of your thoughts and, when necessary, lightning-quick to change them. Well…perhaps not always as on top of your thoughts as you may have wished. And…well, not always so fast on your feet either. But, as you practice toward mastery, you find you're changing.

Having seen all aspects of yourself, including your dark, hidden parts, you're wide awake, conscious of your energy, emotional well-being, and the power you hold. Dozing off again is no longer possible.

"That my creative life is intrinsic to my being comforts me both because I don't have to be afraid of losing it and because I always have a place to turn for solace."

"Having passed the self-doubt and insecurity associated with worrying about being a good enough writer, now I write primarily for self-enjoyment."

What are you more aware of about your creative life, now that you've reached the end?

_____

_____

_____

_____

_____

_____

What are you more aware of about your overall life—something you may have been oblivious to before—now that you've reached the end?

_____

_____

_____

_____

_____

TRANSFORMATION

Whether your completed piece hangs in your own study or a famous art gallery, or is enjoyed by one or one million, your creativity means something. Whether washed away by the tide or remembered as a masterpiece, what you produce reflects your respect for the creative process by faithfully showing up through the productive times and the not-so-productive times.

You followed your imagination and plotted plan and have been rewarded in ways you're only now beginning to appreciate. Was it the completion that contributed to your growth? Or did those internal changes come from the constant stream of love and support you felt by embracing your duel nature through chanting your spiritual pledge? The two tiers come together to create changes that go on without end as you evolve, mature, and grow wiser, more peaceful, and joyful.

Now, the question is, how dramatic and thorough are those internal character changes? In other words, have you been truly transformed? Are your attributes and perceptions changed in depth? Only time will tell. Change is represented by the replacement of an old, limited belief with a broad new one, a newly acquired skill, a mystery solved. Transformation is change at a fundamental spiritual level.

One way to show transformation is by how you deal with dark emotions, difficult people, uncomfortable situations, trials, and setbacks. To be conscious when you're in the grip of unexamined, fear-based beliefs represents change. When you no longer require practice acting in ways that nurture your spirit represents actual transformation.

One Final Confrontation

After all the reversals you've faced during this cycle of creativity, customarily one final clash awaits. However, now, even if all the major forces come together against you, you demonstrate your new awareness, skill, strength, belief, and personal power, and prevail.

And, if you don't, and instead give in to fear and anxiety, anger and outbursts, you get a reaction—either through your body as an illness, rash, cough, ache, or pain, or as a sign in nature. Any sort of feedback is an attempt to pull you back into your true power and remind you of your intuition, imagination, creativity, wisdom, and strength.

Keep learning from your emotions.

What are you feeling right now?

_____

_____

Of the three primary emotions—fear (afraid something bad will happen), sadness (sensing that something bad already has happened), and happiness—where does how you're feeling right now originate?

Fear   Sadness   Happiness

If you circled either fear or sadness, accept your feelings as messengers with clues about what you're here to learn. Explore the deeper meaning of your feelings while at the same time actively choosing to be happy.

You appreciate all that happened to break open your heart and return ownership of your life to you. No one and nothing holds authority over you. Or, if you lose energy, each time, you bounce back more quickly. Be particularly vigilant of what you say to yourself during times of stress. When you're under pressure and things turn difficult, it's easy to regress and revert back to old behaviors and thoughts and beliefs.

Having faced your fear, you find you're no longer afraid. No one has the power to hurt you, because you no longer give anyone license to your power. No longer silenced or dismissive of your goals, dreams, and desires, you trust yourself to go deeper and further. You no longer fear change. You honor your creativity by consistently showing up, eager to voice your inner authority through your art.

Write about a time when everything went smoothly, and you felt optimistic, in control, and full of enthusiasm.

_____

_____

_____

_____

_____

Describe how you feel and act when you fully own your personal power.

_____

_____

_____

_____

_____

Write about a time you gave away some or all of your personal power and authority over your life to limiting beliefs, bad habits, or the safety of prescribed limits and boundaries—when you allowed someone else to influence the direction of your choices or you felt you needed to ask for permission to do what you please.

_____

_____

_____

_____

_____

Describe how you feel and act when you are your powerless self.

_____

_____

_____

_____

_____

You have lost so much—in some cases, all you have. You've also gained the world. You appreciate your weaknesses and your vulnerabilities and no longer look outside for validation and love. You've learned to surround yourself in light…

Write or draw the end of your life or the rolling credits of your personal story.

_____

_____

_____

_____

_____

_____

_____

You're healed when you look back with gratitude even for the dark and scary times.

A SPIRITUAL STATE OF BEING

Along with a new title, you, the initiated, are presented with three gifts to enhance your creative journey. Joy—a sense of enjoyment and urgency flows into all you create. Peace—at peace with what you're creating, you surrender to the process. Love—trusting the gifts, you infuse love in all you create.

As you became more in touch with your inner life and in control of your thoughts and emotions, you began a shift from you usual state of mind toward an awakened state of being. All along, you've been sailing toward "the prize." You thought you were heading toward the completion of your creativity goal. The true prize is the ability to access new states of being at will.

Joy, peace, and love are the modalities of conscious creating. The actions you take count less than the quality of your being while creating. Caressed from within by a sense of spiritual well being, you lighten up, calm down, let go, unwind, relax, and open to the mystery. You're experiencing a spiritual state of being.

A spiritual state of being differs from an emotion and is not the same as a state of mind.

Emotions. Fear, happiness, and sadness are primary human emotions. Emotions come and go as live energy strives to perpetuate itself through havoc, seduction, delight, and bewilderment. Emotion serves a vital purpose in our lives. As foghorns warn sailors to stay clear of the rocks and shoals, primary emotions point you in the direction of healing and smooth sailing.

State of mind. A state of mind is your attitude, outlook, perspective, approach, or mind-set in the moment. Your state of mind reflects your mood, thinking, and mental state or status—internal parts of you addressed throughout this program. Your state of mind is often driven by ego.

Spiritual state of being. Your spiritual state of being is the energetic quality of your spirit in the moment. Spiritual states of being reflect the intensity of peace, love, and joy you feel and radiate out into the world. Creating while in a state of being versus, say, a state of mind connects you to your higher self. When in a state of being, you create something bigger, deeper, and more truthful. Creative empowerment rushes into your work. What's most extraordinary is what you end up with came through you into form and out into the world.

Living with awareness lifts you out of your state of mind. A strong spiritual state of being doesn't so much separate you from your emotions and body as it connects you beyond the physical and temporal and conditional illusions that surround us. When the quality of your spiritual state of being is pure, intuition, inner knowing, and unconditional trust lift you from the mundane and support your spiritual and creative growth in ways you may never have anticipated.

A state of being is driven by spirit.

Peace, Love, Joy

The energetic makeup of your spirit is peace, love, and joy. Peace, love, and joy are spiritual wonders with the power to fill both you and your art with light. Even if what you're creating is born of darkness, an inner light glows bright.

Peace seems the antithesis of fear; joy, a more intense form of happiness; and love, the absence of sorrow. However, fear, happiness, and sorrow originate from external factors influencing our earliest need for survival. Love, peace, and joy, on the other hand, transcend what happens on the outside and reside inside as your birthright. Love, peace, and joy feed the fire within and infuse you with vital healing power.

PEACE

Peace is emotional freedom. Approach any situation with inner tranquility, and you transmit the strength of your spirit, which shifts the quality of the energy around you. Peace allows you to appreciate all aspects of your life and emotions for bringing you to this precise moment. Peace is the purification of mental, physical, and emotional energies. With peace come patience, acceptance, and trust.

What does peace mean to you?

_____

_____

_____

_____

_____

Generally, how peaceful is your life?

Tumultuous   *Fluctuates wildly*   *Even keel*   *Calm*   *Peaceful*

Do you find a connection between the quality of your work and productivity when you're feeling peaceful versus when you're in your head?

Yes   *No*

If you answered yes, what is the connection?

_____

_____

_____

_____

_____

What most contributes to peace in your daily life?

_____

_____

_____

_____

_____

What steps can you take to create more peace in your life?

_____

_____

_____

_____

_____

What skills must your rediscover and develop inside to access peace?

_____

_____

_____

_____

What do you truly want in life?

_____

_____

_____

What steps must you take to get to what you want?

_____

_____

_____

_____

_____

LOVE

When we love unconditionally, we allow creative energy to free flow. The veil between you and your spirit and all others drops. Healing requires love, especially the love and care you show yourself.

True love is unconditional, compassionate, generous, gentle, and kind; it is an open heart filled with trust. Love is like a purifying, bottomless caldron that transmutes fear and sorrow into joy and peace. Love breaks down fixed and toxic emotional burdens connected to past events and clears your way to vitality and healing.

How much love do you receive in your life?

_____

_____

_____

_____

How much love do you give out in your life?

_____

_____

_____

_____

What do you love about living your best creative life?

_____

_____

_____

_____

What steps can you take to create more love in and around your creativity?

_____

_____

_____

_____

JOY

The words "joy" and "happiness" are often used interchangeably, though they have defining differences. Happiness is temporary, and its limited power is rooted in external conditions. Joy, on the other hand, is a state of being, conditional to nothing, and resides inside you. Joy is achieved when you identify secondary emotions that erupt, dig to the primary emotion, and trust in its truth and in your own innate wisdom to solve, overcome, and benefit from whatever comes your way.

With a sense of joy, we regain our balance and reason and a greater perspective that encompasses the wider picture of all of life and the indescribable than simply what is found on the physical plane. Our sense of safety and security is no longer rooted in externalities. Joy brings with it clarity and direction and the energy of wisdom and grace.

How much joy do you experience in your life currently?

None   *Some*   *Heaps*   *A superabundance*

What most contributes to a sense of joy in your life?

_____

_____

_____

_____

_____

What part of living your best creative life brings you joy?

_____

_____

_____

_____

The Best Version of Yourself

In states of joy, love, and peace, you become the best version of yourself. Rather than emotions driving virtually every decision you make, now you make choices that serve your highest good.

Spiritual wonders are always accessible because peace, love, and joy live inside and are always ready for you to activate. You are the veil. Your suffering—what wraps you in drama, fumes on one side. On the other await the fundamental states of being. Embodying these sacred attitudes toward your creativity allows you to touch again the eternal peace, unconditional love, and constant joy you felt before the world tamed you into what you should feel and who you should be.

THE FIRE WITHIN

Is what really counts an end result defined by our current culture—financial gain, fame, and notoriety? What does that say about all the hours of creating alone with nothing but your imagination and a willingness to try without any guarantee of money or renown?

We each have a fire burning within us, a longing. Our spirit is our aliveness, spurs us into action, and inspires us to grow. Trouble is, all too often, fear and sadness blanket our fire. Our desire smolders. Old fears of humiliation, criticism, cumulative shaming, fear of getting caught, exposed as inferior, and lacking block your energy.

Often we inflict hurt or harm and take out revenge against ourselves for not being perfect. Perfection is not the point of our time here on earth. My mother symbolized that belief by always integrating a flaw in the pieces she created.

Return to the fundamentals and, yet again, clear away the flotsam of old patterns and self-destructive habits, rules you've learned and emotions you've assumed. Find and then release stories of hurt and disappointment. You may never completely forget your transgressions or other people's cruelty, but one day, with no authority over you left, the past no longer hurts.

TURN TO MOTHER EARTH

Hold in your mind a story you've told yourself about your unworthiness or flaws. Allow the story to drift through your heart, your belly, and your legs, then out of the soles of your feet and into the ground. Mother Earth composts pain into new life.

Each time you practice quieting your mind and silencing the repetitive and toxic stories, you move nearer to the day when you create more joyfully and open-heartedly than you ever believed possible.

TAKE ACTION

As you've practiced the power of affirmation, the story you've been chained to for years—rusting your heart and weakening your joints—finally ends. Your spiritual pledge has rewritten the story of your life.

Look back at the beginning of the workbook for the first spiritual affirmation you created and chanted. Reward yourself for the changes you've made. Consider what's left to work on.

Rewrite your spiritual mantra, incorporating spiritual states of being to take forward as you imagine, plan, and plot your next creativity goal.

_____

_____

_____

_____

And the Cycle Begins Again

THE UNIVERSAL STORY

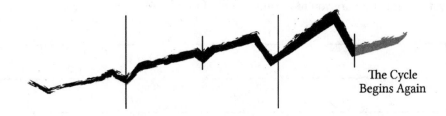

The Cycle
Begins Again

In triumph, you dance on the highest peak of the Universal Story. Then, as the moon slips into the Sea of Creativity and the sun sends out a golden light, you stumble home, crawl in bed, and drop off into a deep sleep.

The energy of the Universal Story drops off, too. Unlike the last downward plummet that fell to such an unnerving low, where you are now represents the sum of all your choices and actions over the last month. The cycle of change winds down before another mystical odyssey sweeps you off on another creativity adventure.

What internal changes have you made?

_____

_____

_____

_____

_____

_____

What external changes have you made?

_____

_____

_____

_____

_____

How have you rewarded (or are you rewarding) yourself for the inner changes you've made?

_____

_____

_____

_____

What's left to work on?

_____

_____

_____

_____

Create a new spiritual pledge.

_____

_____

_____

As you continue creating, and the deeper you dive, the more issues you discover need healing. Some old habits and beliefs are like barnacles stubbornly attached to you. And, as you've learned, with confidence and resolve, you have the strength to pry them loose.

But, for now, rest. Restore. Refresh and renew. As you let go of this particular cycle and invite in a new creativity goal to cycle through the four phases of the Universal Story, you have a new self-awareness. Not by being self-absorbed and selfish, you achieved insights into your emotions and patterns through self-respect and self-love. The more you innovate, the deeper the connection runs with your spirit.

ESSENTIAL GIFTS

Having embraced creativity, the energy of your life rises in significance. Because you've proven your dedication to create and your trustworthiness to go the distance, inspiration appears in every aspect of your life. It's as if the energy of the Universal Story longs to manifest through creativity and, having found an eager spirit, partners with you to create your best creative life.

Energized and excited, you're capable of doing anything you set out to do. Thanks to creativity, your artistic eye and maker's hands, you see and feel tiny miracles everywhere. You slow down and appreciate a blue-sky morning and the star-filled night.

The steps and exercises you've completed bring comfort and an appreciation of the infinite wisdom to support your unique creative expression. You examined your emotional and spiritual life from all angles. Your heart wrenched open to reintroduce you to your spirit. You learned your strengths and discovered abilities you never knew you had. The exercises were a gentler version of picking you up by the heels and shaking off layers of responsibility and expectations, seriousness and fear, and then dousing you in ice-cold water to jolt you awake.

You've reunited with essential gifts you were born with but lost along the way, thinking them insignificant or unimportant in your pursuit of other people's goals. Freed from the burdens you've accumulated throughout your life, the experience feels like meeting yourself again for the first time.

Your surroundings change to better reflect who you are now. On the Universal Story, you're at a time of showing what the world looks like now that you've brought a work of art into being. At each challenge, you broke through barriers. Continue to make time to retreat and reconnect to your spirit. Leave the noise of the world around you—the words and stories and logic and gossip, the mind. Move beyond the drama of emotions. In the quiet, thrive in the spiritual states of being of peace, love, and joy.

THE FUTURE

We live creatively not only for ourselves. We create for the sake of our spirit, family, friends, fans, and other people, Mother Earth and the world at large. As you continue creating and unearthing productive and counterproductive beliefs, you begin to remember the covenant you made before incarnating and then promptly forgot in the chaos of birth. Your backstory wound reflects what you came here to heal.

Do you know your life's purpose?   Yes   No

If you answered yes, what do you believe you're meant to do here on earth?

_____

_____

_____

_____

_____

If you answered no, has the work you've done throughout the program brought you nearer to knowing?

Yes   No

Awed by creativity's power to reconnect you to your spirit, and amazed at all you've learned, you're drawn to use your creativity for activism and the good of the whole—teaching workshops, coming up with innovative ideas of how to rid plastics from choking the sea, sharing a creative life experience.

> "If I'm creating (stories, art, songs—you name it, anything), I feel like myself. I feel alive and true with clear purpose. I get to actually do something greater and larger than myself being the best me."

> "I started only 50 percent successful at writing every day before engaging in social media and getting depressed and angry. Now I'm at 100 percent, relieved and grateful for the quiet internal time I get to spend alone."

The energy of the Universal Story appears to travel in a straight up and down linear pattern. As you've experienced, this isn't exactly the way creativity works. Living your best creative life means being surrounded by a swirl of ideas, irregular currents of productivity, half-finished stories, dried-up paints, dead-ends, and tucked-away projects you circle back around and finish later.

> "I'm always trying new things. I've got so many projects in the works now, I've got to tackle them first!"

YOUR CREATIVE PROCESS

Once you find your creative stride, you never really lose it. Especially now, thanks to your thirty-day deadline. The language of your spirit and the Universal Story are imprinted in your body and mind.

Have you found a rhythm to your days that nurtures your creativity?   **Yes**   **No**

If no, what will help? What do you need that you're missing?

_____

_____

_____

_____

_____

_____

Try creating at different times of the day and night until you settle into a schedule that works best for you. As you learn to listen to your intuition and inner wisdom, give yourself permission to wander off your plan. You now know the difference between what's best for the piece versus creating confusion, procrastination, and setting yourself up for defeat.

Sure, there will be times when you lose your passion and give up what you start. Too many times, however, and a quit-before-you-see-it-to-the-end habit forms. Besides, no matter how wretched or pointless what you're working on, only at the end, with the serenity of detachment, do you have an awakened understanding of what the piece symbolizes. The end is where spiritual wisdom is revealed and awareness leads to change. No matter what, just don't quit.

What you create comes from a mystical place—your imagination. Together, you and your imagination and your spirit shape an idea, a line of dialogue, or a note into something others can see, taste, hear, smell, and touch. What comes out of your collaboration may not look, taste, sound, smell, or feel how you initially envisioned. Typically, the wisp of an idea doesn't reveal itself in totality. There it goes. And, now, here it is again…

LIVING YOUR BEST CREATIVE LIFE

Even after dropping all attachments to family and friends and reconnecting to love and compassion for each of them and all of Mother Nature and the world around me, I still sometimes wonder how I got here. I've had several books published and enjoyed international success. Writing this book has been an entirely unique experience.

This is me now, who I am, having consciously traveled many times through each phase of the Universal Story. I've written about the Universal Story for more than twenty years. When I started, more often than not, I'd reach to pin down an ethereal energetic aspect of the Universal Story only to have it evaporate and vanish. Each attempt becomes yet another opportunity to solidify that which is of the spirit. Breaking down each step to share with you has further enriched my appreciation for the mystical rhythmic energy in my own life.

The one question I continually return to is this: do you have to go through a dark night and lose everything, and mostly yourself, before you earn entrance into living your best creative life? For me, my pain and my hopes and dreams in my past and the future connect to a far greater reality. Touching my own suffering connects me to the suffering of all others.

Every form of creativity is a spiritual pursuit that restores our forgotten belief in possibilities and the miraculous. The more times you wade into the unknown and learn through experience, the more likely you are to overcome all the challenges you face in life.

Keep taking risks and discovering what you're capable of and how strong you are. Endowed with wisdom and a deep state of bliss, you understand that taking the first step forward into a new beginning is to travel fully awake and alert for lessons on way to your dreams.

Dreams come true through taking action.

THE UNIVERSAL STORY

The Universal Story is a pattern of cosmic energy through time and space that exists within and throughout your life. Notice how the line at the end that connotes the start of the new beginning is higher than the beginning where we first met. The energy of your life has shifted higher and burns hotter because of all you've learned, all you've struggled with, your risks, and all you've mastered.

The Universal Story is in the undercurrent of every breath you take, every story you tell yourself, and all of nature. Learn to refer to the Universal Story when you consider new goals or when, having tried, you find yourself mired and lost or simply curious about where you are and where you are headed or, at least, the general direction in which you are moving.

YOUR NEXT CREATIVITY GOAL

A vast new horizon of possibilities and wonder spreads across the Sea of Creativity. Begin daydreaming about your next creativity goal. Roll up the Universal Story for your first project and set it aside. Draw a new Universal Story for a new creativity goal. Tuck away this workbook and begin a new one. Learning to listen and be guided by your spirit is developmental. What I mean is that you're only able to grasp what you're developmentally ready to understand. Therefore, each time through the workbook deepens your readiness to glean yet more of the layers of complexity in the text toward mastery as you further develop your relationship with your spirit. Each workbook then becomes a keepsake journal beyond the art you produce to mark your progress through layers of emotions and thoughts and beliefs. If you'd like your next creativity goal to be more reflective of you, try the following.

First, think back to two or more scenes from your past (near or far, intense or mundane) clearly woven in your memory, as if they just took place. Write down details you remember.

First Memory

_____

_____

_____

_____

_____

Second Memory

_____

_____

_____

_____

_____

Next, identify the main idea, underlying meaning, or themes in the memories that flicker at you. For example, when I preform the exercise, elements of communication and finding my voice always come up. Choose the most prevalent such as friendship, courage, change, justice, alienation, revenge, faith, loyalty, acceptance, perseverance, betrayal, honesty, cooperation, intimidation, deception, temptation, rescue, loneliness, truth, abandonment, or ambition.

List any recurring themes.

_____

_____

_____

_____

How do the themes resemble each other?

_____

_____

What do the themes mean to you and how do they represent you?

_____

_____

Now, use your imagination for ideas of how to incorporate one or more of your themes into your next project. For instance, post an entire photography series on Instagram that embraces and highlights some aspect of your themes.

MARK THE END

Sunrise breaks on the horizon. Still spring waters reveal the depths of the sea. From a kelp forest, a sea otter pup chirps for its mother. Before you move on and begin a new workbook for your next creativity project, first, mark the end of this cycle.

Today's Date   _____

TAKE ACTION

After you're rested and are ready to create something new, decide on an external creativity goal. This may be an entirely new goal based on the exercise above, something that came to you in the middle of the night, or yet another part of the larger goal you broke into parts at the beginning of the program. Because creativity is such a powerful therapeutic tool to express the unspeakable, if you have a backstory wound that won't stop oozing pain, consider a goal that affords you another means to heal yourself.

Ready to begin again?

I'm with you in spirit…

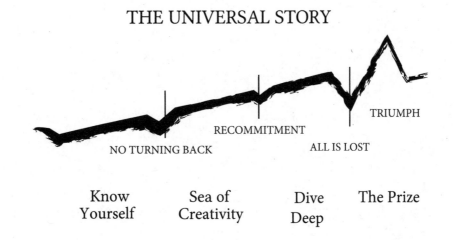

THE UNIVERSAL STORY

Acknowledgments

As I prepare to cross the threshold to my next grand adventure, I first want to extend my thanks. I'm grateful for each of you who have reached out a hand of support to me. Thank you, Peter Archer, for your early help pulling my ideas of the Universal Story down to earth. Thank you, Jill Corcoran, for remembering and then finding the book the perfect home. Thank you, Elizabeth Hollis Hansen, for seeing the promise and your help and support shaping the book into the form it is today. Thank you, Jennifer Holder and Jennifer Eastman, for your input and suggestions. To everyone at New Harbinger Publications, thank you for giving me the opportunity to solidify my ideas and my own personal healing through writing *Boundless Creativity*.

Deepest gratitude to Joseph Campbell, the first man after my father I ever loved.

And thank you, Caroline Myss, for your brilliance. Thank you Louise Hay for your wisdom.

Over the many years I've interacted with other creatives, I've been humbled by the trust shown me. Thanks to each of you who have so openly shared your deepest hopes and dreams, fears and pain while attempting to live your best creative life. I'm filled with gratitude for having witnessed your courage and openhearted commitment to your creativity.

And, to you who have stuck with me since the beginning of my spiritual journey by way of showing up for my talks and workshops and intensives and retreats, buying my books and videos, writing reviews and sending emails, thank you. Thank you, Michelle of Fresh Designs for creating the illustrations. Thank you, Jan Shaw, for supporting me in my very first transformational workshop from which *Boundless Creativity* grew and evolved. And special thanks goes out to Bobby Ray for your belief and support.

Lastly, I want to thank each and every one of you generous spirits who completed one or more surveys and answered my endless questions. Thank you.

This book is a love letter to you and anyone ready to live his or her best creative life.

See you on the other side…

Martha
marthaalderson.com

Martha Alderson, MA, has been exploring and writing about plot and creativity for more than thirty years, and helping writers develop plot and structure, character transformation and change, and pin down universal elements and dynamics in stories and life. Her work supporting children and adults with their writing quickly evolved into plotting a course of action for anyone looking to enrich their lives through embarking on a spiritual odyssey to higher creativity. Author of *The Plot Whisperer*, along with several other books of fiction and nonfiction, Alderson works with bestselling authors, New York editors, Hollywood directors, artists, and performers from all over the world. She also leads transformational workshops, book groups, and retreats for people privately and through her popular online program, where she helps people enliven their creativity, tap into inspiration to uncover their ambitions, and better envision imaginative solutions as they work toward realizing their goals. Alderson lives in Santa Cruz, CA.

Real change *is* possible

For more than forty-five years, New Harbinger has
published proven-effective self-help books and pioneering
workbooks to help readers of all ages and backgrounds
improve mental health and well-being, and achieve lasting
personal growth. In addition, our spirituality books
offer profound guidance for deepening awareness and
cultivating healing, self-discovery, and fulfillment.

Founded by psychologist Matthew McKay and Patrick
Fanning, New Harbinger is proud to be an independent,
employee-owned company. Our books reflect our
core values of integrity, innovation, commitment,
sustainability, compassion, and trust. Written by leaders
in the field and recommended by therapists worldwide,
New Harbinger books are practical, accessible, and
provide real tools for real change.

newharbingerpublications

MORE BOOKS for the SPIRITUAL SEEKER

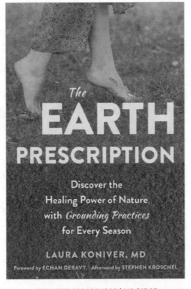

ISBN: 978-1684034895 | US $17.95

ISBN: 978-1608820313 | US $16.95

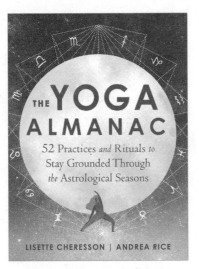

ISBN: 978-1684034352 | US $17.95

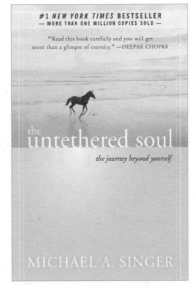

ISBN: 978-1572245372 | US $17.95

newharbingerpublications

NON-DUALITY PRESS | REVEAL PRESS